How Does God Speak to Us?

Discerning the Voice of God in your Daily Life

Nicole Murray

COPYRIGHT

DEDICATION

For the One who was, and is, and is to come.

CONTENTS

PREFACE

I want to tell you how I was led to write this book. I manage a prayer ministry and we do prophetic words as the Lord gives them to us. I'm a firm believer that God does speak to His children and that anyone of us can receive prophetic words from Him.

The purpose of the prophetic word is not to add to anything already written in scripture but to encourage, build up the body of Christ, warn the people of God and give insight into future events all while staying in line with what is written in the scriptures (1 Corinthians 14:3).

I generally receive a prophetic word from the Lord at least once per month and they are directed to the body of Christ. You should know that I do not consider myself a prophet; however, I do have the gift of prophesy.

Around May 2019, I noticed that the prophetic words were starting to slow down and I was not receiving them with the same frequency as I did in the past. God didn't have anything new to say. While I was still receiving words from

Him concerning my personal life, there was no message given for the body of Christ as a whole. There were months when I received nothing. I asked Him after awhile what was going on, why wasn't I receiving any more prophetic words for the body of Christ?

He told me that He wanted me to teach the people how to hear from Him themselves.

When He said that, I knew that something was coming where people needed to hear God for themselves. I figured it was possible there would be a few false prophets here and there and perhaps some leaders in the church that would fall into some kind of sin and the people needed to know how to seek God for directions and answers.

I had no idea what was about to happen.

All during the time when God was silent, I would still see messages from the Lord from many different prophetic voices. It was puzzling to me because I didn't understand where they were getting them from. Please understand this doesn't mean that God can't speak to someone else and not give the information to me. He can do whatever He wants to do. I just found it strange that no one else was saying or hearing what I was hearing. They were all just "cranking out" these prophetic messages at the same level of frequency.

Upon a closer look I noticed that there was nothing new about the messages but it was more of a regurgitation of past messages just being repeated over and over again. You know…"God is going to bless you this year" "This is your year" "You're getting double for your trouble this year" But I saw no one saying that God was slowing down on the messages and wanted them to teach the people how to hear for themselves.

I marveled at the fact that sometimes we can get into the flow of things and miss when the Holy Spirit has removed His presence from it.

In November 2019, in obedience to what the Lord said, I taught my first class on the subject and then the Lord told me to do another one in February 2020.

Then in March 2020 COVID-19 hit and we were all on lockdown. And it was at that moment when I started to get the picture that this was more than just a few random false prophets where people needed to protect themselves.

This was about the entire church of Jesus Christ knowing how to connect with their Savior and King personally. Knowing how to hear from Him personally without the pastor, or the prayer team, or the worship team or anybody else giving instructions.

It was bigger than what I expected.

Then with the United States elections in full swing and all these prophetic voices coming out with prophecies of what God told them, coupled with the greatest divide we have ever seen in the church, it became even more evident that now more than ever we needed to hear God for ourselves. We can't rely on our leaders anymore. What if they are wrong? Should you wear a mask or not? Should you take the vaccine or not? Should you defy the authority and go to church or not?

The truth is, only GOD can answer those questions concerning the health and well being of you and your loved ones.

What if what they are telling you is based solely on their own desires? How would you know? The only way is to hear God for yourself.

That's why I wrote this book.

I pray that through this book not only will you get drawn into a closer relationship with Jesus Christ, but also your ears would be opened to hearing His voice.

Chapter 1

Prayer

Prayer: this is where it starts.

So, it's my favorite thing because, really, prayer is basically talking to God. That's what it is. It is just having a conversation with your Lord and your Savior and your King. And it's such a simple thing.

But a lot of people don't do it. They don't do enough of it. I think it is intimidating for some people because they don't understand it. They don't know how it works. They don't know if they are doing it right or wrong. So they just tend to stay away from it.

I want to clear all that up for you and by the end of this book make you feel comfortable enough to approach the Lord and talk to Him about whatever it is you want to talk to Him about with confidence.

Okay, so let's dive in.

Prayer is simply just talking to God. And believe it or not, God does talk back to you. A lot of people believe that this kind of communication either can't happen, or in order for you to hear from God, you need to have some kind of spiritual gift that's given to some Christians but not to others. Well, that's simply not true.

Psalm 145:18 "The Lord is near to all who call on Him, to all who call on Him in truth."

It is not a gift. It is a right, as a son or daughter of the King, to hear from your Father and He wants to speak to you. But I think we are not taught this. People come to not believe it. They think it can't happen. Or it can't happen because they belong to a certain denomination that doesn't really talk about the ability that we all can actually hear from God.

They never realize that this is possible.

So, what I'm going to do is tell you my story and them I'm going to use it to hopefully inspire you to do the same thing; to go to the Lord and talk to Him.

I got saved in a conservative church, a Presbyterian church that believes that the only way the Lord speaks to you is through the bible, by reading the scriptures.

This is true. God does speak to you through reading the bible. It's just not the only way that He speaks. There are many, many, many ways in which the Lord speaks. You do want to start with the bible. It's very important to do that because when the Lord does begin to speak to you, you will know that it's not your voice or the voice of the enemy. The only way to discern that, or to differentiate that, is by reading the word of God because then the word becomes the barometer that tells you this is God or it's not God, it doesn't sound like God or it sounds like something God would say.

Psalm 130:21 "…heeding the voice of His word."

That's why it's so important for you to read the bible, and yes, He does speak to you through the bible.

But you can hear God. You can hear God audibly. This is not a very common thing, but He does speak audibly.

Isaiah 30:21 "And your ears shall hear a word behind you saying, "This is the way, walk in it." When you turn to the right or turn to the left."

He speaks into your spirit which sometimes can feel like He is speaking right into your chest. Or He can speak to you through you just knowing. You will just get a sense of knowing something and it didn't come from you. It's a source outside of yourself.

Romans 8:14-16 "For as many as are led by the Spirit of God, these are sons of God. For you did not receive the spirit of bondage again to fear, but you received the Spirit of adoption by whom we cry out, "Abba,ᴵ Father." The Spirit Himself bears witness with our spirit that we are children of God,"

There are many different ways He speaks. And He speaks a lot through your senses, your five spiritual senses. While you have natural senses, you also have spiritual senses. He may speak through those senses and that is how you will know it's Him. This whole process starts with prayer, which is just a simple conversation with the Lord. It's taking time to sit and talk to Him. As with any conversation, no one likes to talk to someone that is always dominating the conversation, always talking and talking, someone who never stops to hear what you have to say and to listen.

Luke 6:27a NIV "But to you who are listening, I say..."

The speaking is just as important as the listening for what He's saying. So when you sit to pray, you need to ask the Lord for whatever it is that you are going to ask Him for, or just to talk to Him, and then you need to be quiet. Listen.

You don't need to have worship music going on or the Christian TV in the background or anything else going on. Just quiet, where you can actually hear Him and He will speak to you.

Believe me. I'll go into that more. It's the speaking and the listening. It's very important.

Now a little bit about me and when I came to know the Lord. I just always knew from the very beginning that He's alive. All of us came into this world as broken human beings. We all inherited the sinful nature of Adam and Eve. There's no one walking around on earth that doesn't have a sin problem.

Romans 3:23 *"for all have sinned and fall short of the glory of God,"*

Therefore, God knowing that we needed a solution to this problem, put on flesh and came to earth as a man. That is Jesus. Jesus is actually God in bodily form who came to dwell among men. He came so that He could pay for our sins upon the cross when He died. It costs us nothing; but it cost Him everything.

John 3:16-17 *"For God so loved the world that He gave His only begotten Son, that whoever believes in Him should not perish but have everlasting life. For God did not send His Son into the world to condemn the world, but that the world through Him might be saved."*

In receiving Christ's death upon the cross for our sins, we are then grafted into the family of God. We become a son or a daughter of God.

Christ died and He resurrected on the third day. He went into heaven and sits at the right hand of the Father, making intercessions for us. We also know that God is a Spirit. We have read many stories throughout the bible that He speaks to man. We also know that when we receive Christ and we receive the Holy Spirit, the Holy Spirit comes to live within us, which means that the alive, living God deposits Himself within us.

Romans 8:14 "For as many as are led by the Spirit of God, these are sons of God."

That means the living God dwells within us by His Holy Spirit. There is a connection between us and Him. Now knowing this, why wouldn't He speak to you if you're His child? Of course, He wants to speak with you. It's just getting into the habit of having that conversation.

Your connection was establish in accepting Christ as your Savior and then the Holy Spirit living within you is like someone taking a lamp that was once unplugged and plugging it in. The Spirit of God brings illumination to the word of God and also to the things of God and how God will speak to you. The Holy Spirit upon dwelling in you, activated your spiritual senses.

For me, what I did at the very beginning was I would get home, I was single at the time so I had the house to myself and I could just speak openly without people looking at me like I was crazy. I still do it to this day and my daughter knows. She is like, 'Oh, you're talking to God again.' Because I will just be there talking away. Yes, out loud. I would tell Him about my day, my whole day, what happened to me. Now we all know that God goes with you wherever you are, but it was great for me to just come home and offload, talk about whatever I needed to talk about that was going on at work. It's far better to share your problems with God than with others. All His advice and solutions work!

He's like a friend; tell him what's going on! So I talked to Him and I would get everything out. You know it's amazing, sometimes we almost have to hear ourselves say something to understand what's going on. Does that ever happen to you? It's like you could have a dream or something and you don't have full understanding of it until you actually express it, verbally.

So when I speak to Him, and it comes out and I hear myself saying some of the things that I am saying, sometimes a revelation even comes from that. Then I remain quiet and continue doing what I'm doing, if I'm making dinner or I'm cleaning the house or whatever I'm doing. I do it silently with nothing on around. Sometimes there would be an extra chair and I'm eating, I would do this in the very beginning, I would just imagine that He was sitting in that chair and I would just talk to Him as I was eating and I continued doing that. Did He speak to me instantly? No.

It went on for about two weeks of me doing that until one morning as I was getting ready for work, I was not speaking, I was just getting dressed and then I heard myself answer a question. Now, if I am going to answer a question, it means someone asked me a question. At that moment, when it happened, I thought to myself, 'Okay, that's odd.' You know what's amazing (and this will happen to you)? The first time He starts speaking to you, you will literally go, "Oh my goodness, this is happening!" It's like you expect it, you want it, but then when it happens, you're like 'okay, this is really happening.' So I answered the question, I don't remember what it was, and I stopped and thought, 'Okay, that was really odd.' I kept doing what I was doing and I kind of brushed it off, but not really.

The next day, the same thing happened, I was getting dressed for work again, and I had another question which I answered the second time. When I did it, and I realized this was not a fluke, it happened yesterday and it happened again today, that's when I realized, He's talking back to me now. He's actually speaking. God is always speaking, but it may take a while for you to recognize how He is speaking to you. Once you discern the way he speaks, you'll find it much easier to hear Him all the time. We're now engaging, now we're dialoguing. When I answered the question instead of stopping talking, I continued speaking to Him and this is what started the whole conversation back and forth.

Yes! It is truly and seriously that simple. But you have to do it. When you begin to do this it might happen for you instantly or it might take some time. If you are not in a household where you can just openly speak, without people looking at you like you're crazy, you may need to go off somewhere else. You might need to make some time to go somewhere, go for a walk. Maybe there's a place that you can go to in silence and that's where you speak to Him.

But it is something you must do every single day. Just try to make some time to do that. Decide when it is the best time for you to do it. Whatever time is convenient for you. Just make some time. You have to remember, we have the same number of hours in the day as Abraham did, as Moses did, as Joshua did. We really have no excuse. We're the ones that crowd our time with social media and TV and all the other things that come to take our time away from Him. So, it is one of those things where you have to put the time aside, you have to say, 'Okay, I'm spending one hour with God today to praise, to read the bible, to talk to Him. Within that time you're going to have that conversation with Him, you're going to talk and then you're going to give it some time. Fifteen minutes, however much time you have, where you're just listening. You're not saying anything. He will begin to speak to you. This is the simplest, most basic way to do it.

I've taught this to people with 100% success rate. So why not you? When I started this as a new Christian, I did not realize that the people in the church I attended didn't do this. I thought this was how every Christian communicated with God. They believed that He only spoke through the bible. When I would go back and tell them things, they would look at me like, 'What are you talking about?' as if I was strange and the weird one. So I stopped, after a couple times, telling anyone that it was happening because I thought, 'Am I the only one that this is happening with?' I decided not to say anything and kind of stepped back from it. But as my relationship with the Lord grew and grew, I started to talk to Him more and He started talking back to me more. Then, I would be in different prayer meetings or talking to people and I would say things. I would try not to say, 'Oh, God said' or 'the Lord told me this morning'. I would stay away from that and say things like, 'Oh, I kind of get the feeling ...' or 'I think it's possible that God might see it this way...'. I would disguise my comments in this manner.

I think I slipped up a few times because finally one day one of the ladies took me off to the side and said, 'I'm getting the feeling by some of the things that you're saying that you are actually talking to God and He's talking back to you.' I then said to her, 'Yes, I am. And yes, He is'. She said to me, 'How are you doing this? I've been saved for over 20 years and I've never had God talk to me and you're a new believer. You've only been saved for two months and you're talking to God regularly?' I responded, 'Yeah.' So I asked her if she wanted me to show her how to do it. "Yes', was her response. I told her exactly what I'm sharing with you now. I said that's all you have to do. You already read your bible. Talk to Him and He starts talking to you. It might not happen right away, but when it does, believe me, it's like accessing a door.

Jeremiah 29:12-13 "Then you will call on Me and come and pray to Me and I will listen to you. You will seek Me and find Me when you seek Me with all your heart."

You now know the way in the front door. You get in the door and you use the door every single day. I said, 'Once He starts talking, it will not stop. You just have to keep the conversation going every day with Him and whatever instructions He's given you during your time together, you follow those instructions and you go about doing what you need to do, just as He would show it to you'. As you begin to be more obedient to His voice, do the thing that He's telling you to do. He will talk to you more because now He's like, 'This is great! I have a receptive child. I have a child who actually wants to do what I want her or him to do'. He will start talking to you even more. Your relationship will become so strong because He will start to show you things and tell you things. He's not saying it to other people, but He will tell you because He knows that He can trust you. He knows that you're going to do whatever it is He's going to ask you to do.

Not everything He tells you is to be repeated and some things are very delicate and personal information about others. Not that God is a gossip. He is not, but He does this so that you will have a better understanding of why people do the things they do and say what they say. You will be even more compassionate with others when you understand what is really going on in their life. He will show you how to pray for others and what's happening around the world as well.

So, she did it. Somebody who's been saved for over 20 years, and reads here bible almost every day but she never heard God speak to her. You should have seen her about 2 weeks later. I could tell the minute she walked in the door because her face was beaming with excitement and she excitedly said, 'Oh my gosh! It happened! It happened!' I said, 'See, it works! This isn't something that works for some people and not for others.' The bible says signs and wonders are for those who believe. God will show up for you just because you believe Him.

James 1:6 " But let him ask in faith, with no doubting, for he who doubts is like a wave of the sea driven and tossed by the wind"

If you believe, you will receive. The fact that you sit there and you talk to Him every day, don't you think eventually He's going to say, 'Well, I better say something because obviously this child of mine knows that I speak and wants to hear Me'. That is the nature of your Father in heaven. You're not going to ask Him for a fish and He turns around and gives you a stone. This is not His nature.

Luke 11:10 "For everyone who asks receives, and he who seeks finds, and to him who knocks it will be opened."

This is how it works. I did it for her and for many other people. It doesn't matter if you've been saved for a million years, you can start this today. This is such a simple thing that a child can do it and pick up on it very easily. But like I said earlier, the bible becomes your guideline; it becomes what you use to say this is God because of what He has been saying to me. You cannot separate God from His word. Even after He starts speaking to you, you MUST continue reading the bible. Whatever He says MUST be found in the bible.

You never want to stay away from the bible. Somehow, once God starts speaking to you directly, you think, 'Okay, I no longer need to read the bible because now He will just tell me Himself.' It doesn't work like that. You actually need to keep doing both, and you want to add another key element, which is writing it down. Whatever He says to you, write that down; what time and what He said. You might keep a notebook going with your conversations and He's going to love that because He will know that you are a good steward of His voice, that you actually care what He has been saying.

You can start this communing with God by choosing a time that works for you. I find that for me the best time is early in the morning because there's no noise. My day hasn't started, there aren't these things going on in my mind. So when I'm fresh and there's nothing else around, I can talk to Him and I hear more clearly because my mind hasn't started running yet with the day's work or what I have to do.

Have you ever tried sleeping, whether at night or in the morning? Maybe you woke up at 2 o'clock in the morning or 3 o'clock and you can't go back to sleep. You ask yourself, 'Why can't I go back to sleep?'

Guess what? Many times that is God actually wanting to talk to you. Yes, it is! All you have to do is sit up in your bed or go out of your room and just go to a quiet spot where you can be awake instead of falling back asleep in bed.

Luke 5:16 NIV"Jesus often withdrew to lonely places and prayed."

You want to try to be alert and you also want to have your notebook, notepad, or whatever device you use to take your notes. Just say to Him, 'Okay, Lord, what do you want to say to me.' Things will just come to your mind and it will be Him telling you something. You want to write it down. It may be something you will want to pray about.

Many times when we can't sleep, that's God wanting to talk to us but we have to get up and listen and talk with Him, engage Him and pray. Once you do that, I promise you will be back asleep just like that! Sometimes, this is how He gets our attention, by getting us up. Now, we're awake, thinking I don't know why I can't go back to sleep. That's God all right.

I think it may help to think about it this way. Think about someone you admire, whether they're still alive or they've passed on. Anyone that you just think to yourself, 'Boy, I would love to sit down and have lunch with this person or dinner or have coffee and just pick their brain, talk to them about anything'; whether it's a world leader, a president, or somebody that you really admire. Now, imagine one day they call you up and they say, 'Hey, I'd like to invite you to come to my office and we can talk. You're going to say, 'Of course, absolutely I want to come! What time?' If they told you they were going to send a driver for you at 3:30 in the morning, you might think that is kind of early, but you will be there because you are not going to give up the opportunity to go and sit with that person because they are that important to you. You'll get up, wash your face, and put some coffee on if you're going to need that coffee to stay awake. You are going to be ready because you know that driver is going to be there at 3:30. Or you need to be at the airport at 4 o'clock. Whatever it may be, you are going to be there because you want to get to sit with that person who is so important to you and hear what they have to say. So you go to meet with them and they're basically just telling you whatever is on their heart, whatever is on their mind. The more you listen and engage with what they say; they are going to say, 'Great, we should do this again sometime.' So you meet with them again, and the next thing you know, they start telling you a lot about themselves that you didn't know. The same thing happens when the Lord comes to us in the morning to get us up. We have to look at it that way, except this isn't some celebrity or world leader, this is the creator of the universe, this is the God who spoke the world into being, this is the God who can create a human being. No one else can do that. This is the God who does miracles. This is the God who has salvation. This is who's coming to you. I think this is very important for you to understand so that you'll have the same level of reverence and honor when you think about whom it is that's coming to say, 'Get up, I would like to talk to you.' You honor Him by responding in a way that says, 'I know who you are and I am paying attention, I'm going to write down what you say and I'm going to do what you say.'

Jeremiah 33:3 "Call to Me, and I will answer you, and show you great and mighty things, which you do not know

At that moment, He's going to say, 'Okay, let Me show you something cool!' Then He reveals things to you that you will think are mind blowing. You go tell people, if He allows because sometimes it's just between the two of you, this is your secret. Yes, sometimes He does that. Other times, He will allow you to tell people. They'll say, 'Whoa, that's pretty cool. How did you know that?' It's always going to be some knowledge or some understanding that's higher than the human mind. That's what's so wonderful about God; He is above all, everything, El Elyon, the God Most High. He can tell you things and show you things that no one else can and it's the greatest thing in the world.

This is just the beginning stages of prayer. I want to encourage you to go and sit with Him, to talk with Him and have Him talk to you. Write it down. Do what He says. Make time every day, not only to talk to Him but to listen to Him.

Do it, and through this you will start to develop a relationship with Him. You will start hearing from God yourself. You, too, will have the same story that I have, or an even greater story, of speaking to the Almighty God.

***

Personal Reflections:

When you hear the word 'PRAYER', what comes to mind?

Have you ever talked or do you regularly talk with God?

Has your perception of PRAYER changed since reading this information?

Create a SMART goal in regards to the information presented here.

Specific

Measurable

Achievable

Realistic

Time bound

By (set a date) I will have ____minute long conversations with God at ____o'clock every day.

Practical Steps:

1. Repent and ask God to forgive your sins
2. Spend some time praising and worshipping Him
3. Pray, ask Him for what you would like Him to do for you.

4. Sit quietly and wait

If you can do this for about one hour each day you will be sure to hear from the Lord. Every night before you go to bed read the Bible.

***

Prayer:

Abba Father,

Thank you for embracing me as Your child. I thank You that today I am invited to hear from You in many other ways and not just through the bible. I pray that I will know the joy of Your Voice in its many facets and will speak of it with those around me for Your glory, in Jesus name.

Amen

***

Chapter 2

How Does God Speak?

*W*hen we say, 'Someone said' or 'I heard someone say', the first thing you're going to think is hearing with our ears. When someone says, 'God said to me...' we're generally thinking it is something they heard audibly because that's what hearing sounds like to us. I'm here to tell you that in the spiritual realm, when you're dealing with God, or angelic beings, it's really your five spiritual senses that you are using to hear God. You're actually hearing through your five senses; sight, smell, taste, touch, and hearing. Just as you have 5 natural senses, you can actually have all these senses in the realm of the spirit and that is how you are actually hearing God.

I want to share with you some scriptures that point to the fact that it's not just audibly.

Psalm 34:8. 'Oh taste and see that the Lord is good. Blessed is the man who trusts in Him'.

We have sight and we have taste.

Genesis 32:25 "Now when He saw that He did not prevail against him, He touched the socket of his hip; and the socket of Jacob's hip was out of joint as He wrestled with him."

So there is touching that has happened. You may have at one point or another walked into a room and just had the hairs on the back of your neck stand up or you just get a feeling in that room. That's actually your sense of touch that's picking up whatever being or spirit is in the room. You might discern it that way or hear it that way.

Daniel 10:7 "And I, Daniel, alone saw the vision, for the men who were with me did not see the vision; but a great terror fell upon them, so that they fled to hide themselves. "

It says Daniel was the only one that saw the vision. In Daniel Chapter 10, it says an angel came to deliver a message to Daniel and when the angel came, Daniel went into a 'vision' and actually saw it visibly, with his spiritual eyes of course, because it says, 'those who were with me did not see it, but such a terror overwhelmed them that they fled and hid themselves.' No one around him saw anything, this is how we know that he saw it with his spiritual eyes because if it happened in the natural then everyone would've seen it, but instead they felt it. They had their spiritual sense of touch activated. Remember I talked about walking into a room and just feeling that presence? Well, when that angel came into their presence, Daniel saw the vision that no one else saw, but they felt something and ran way.

Song of Solomon 2:1"I am the rose of Sharon, the lily of the valley"

Jesus is referred to as the Rose of Sharon. Just think about that, the smell of a rose.

2 Corinthians 2:15 'For we are to God the fragrance of Christ, among those who are being saved and among those who are perishing.'

We, ourselves as Christians, let off a fragrance that goes up to God. To others around us in the realm of the spirit, people can pick up that there is something about you, and if they can smell in the spirit, they may actually smell you.

I have a friend and we would go places together and she would say to me, 'Do you smell that?' I would say 'no'. She would say, 'It smells like night blooming jasmine'. We would be looking around but there was no jasmine but she would smell it. So we just brushed it off. This happened a few times before it came to me that this was a spiritual sense of smell which God was using to communicate something to her.

She smelled the presence of the Lord as He entered the room. We started to realize whenever we would go out to minister, or whenever she was going anywhere to share the gospel of Jesus Christ or talk about the Lord to someone, He would make known to her that He was there with her by allowing her to smell Him in the spirit.

Jasmine is just one thing. You can smell bad things too, unclean spirits. To me they smell like dirty clothes. I smell laundry that has been sitting there and it needs to be washed, sweaty clothes. That's how it smells to me. Other people will smell the spirit of death and they'll say it smells like formaldehyde. All of these things can happen. Someone can come around you or even be across the room, and you can smell alcohol by looking at them and there is no alcohol in the room. This will be God saying this person has a problem with drinking.

There are all these ways in the realm of the spirit and through our senses that God can actually speak to us. I want you to keep that in mind.

If you start smelling things just pay attention to where and when they happen and who is around. Especially, if no one else seems to be smelling what you are.

I'm fascinated when I talk to people and they say, 'Well, God told me... '. I ask, 'How did He tell you?' That always catches people off guard because they'll say, 'Why would you ask me how did He tell me?' I respond, 'Well, don't you want to know how He is talking to you? If it were me, I would want to know if I'm growing in the things of the Lord by all the different ways that God is communicating with me because now I can *see*, I can *hear*, I can *smell*, I can *taste*, and I can *feel* the touch of the Lord on me. All of these things can happen so I'm always examining His channels of communications. So I ask, 'How did you hear?' because I can tell you not many people hear the audible voice of God. It does not happen often and I've been saved since 2002 and I've only ever heard the audible voice of God one time. Only once, and it was so loud, I looked around the room of about 70 people and I realized none of them heard Him. I was the only one, much like Daniel saw that vision no one else saw. The vision that no one else saw but they all felt the presence.

It is important to understand there are different ways that He speaks and don't believe that God isn't speaking to you because you are not hearing Him audibly. You could be hearing Him through many other ways.

Keeping in mind what I shared about the five spiritual senses, but then also understand that it is layered into the way in which the message comes to you.

The main way in which we all hear God speak to everyone is through the bible, when you read the word of God. That is the first way in which God is speaking to you, reading is your sight. He is speaking through seeing words, or if you're listening to the audio bible, then it's audio.

2 Timothy3:16-17'All scripture is given by inspiration of God and is profitable for doctrine, for reproof, for correction, for instruction and righteousness and so that the man of God may be complete and thoroughly equipped for every good work.'

He is speaking to us and imparting to us instructions by reading the word. He is going to engage with you through His word, then you can move along and you will witness that He speaks in many other ways as well.

The next channel of communication that God speaks to you that I'm going to mention is through situational or circumstantial changes.

1 Kings 17:1-8 'And Elijah, the Tishbite of the inhabitants of Gilead, said to Ahab, 'As the Lord God of Israel lives before whom I stand, there shall not be due nor rain these years except at my word.' Then the word of the Lord came to him saying get away from here and turn eastward and hide by the brook of Cherith, which flows into the Jordan, and it shall be that you shall drink of the brook and I have commanded the ravens to feed you there. So he went and did according to the word of the Lord, for he went and stayed by the brook of Cherith, which flows into the Jordan. The ravens brought him bread and meat in the morning and bread and meat in the evening and he drank form the brook. And it happened that after a while that the brook dried up because there had been no rain in the land. Then the word of the Lord came to him saying, 'Go from this place.'

God goes on to give Elijah instructions.

This is a situational or circumstantial change. I'm going to explain to you what happened. The Lord told Elijah, 'I need you to go to this brook'. He heard God and went to that brook. The Lord told Elijah, 'I'm going to command the ravens to feed you and the brook is there for you to drink from.' So Elijah did as he was commanded by the Lord and all of his needs were met. When God tells you to do something, you do what He tells you. Elijah had food and water. However; soon the birds were not coming with food as often and the water in the brook started drying up. God had not yet spoken to him but that was a sign, God put Elijah on notice that change was coming. What I mean when I say situational or circumstantial is you can look at what is going on around you. God doesn't have to come right out and say this is what's happening. You should be able to discern by your environment that change is coming. Elijah noticed when the brook started to dry up and he said, 'Okay, this is changing. Then after a while, God came and spoke to Elijah and He gave him instructions but Elijah was already put on notice that, the way in which God was supplying for his need was about to change.' The situation around him was changing and this put him in a place where he was already waiting to hear about his next move.

God will do the same thing with us as well. He may not say it right away but the minute we see that things start changing "the brook is starting to dry up" this means get ready for a change.

When we spend time with God and we're hearing from him, we don't need to get all nervous when things start changing. He will tell us. But we need to be aware of what's going on around us so that we are not caught off guard.

Another way God speaks to us is through *peace.*

Colossians 3:15 'Let your heart be always guided by the peace of the Anointed One.'

He called you to peace as a part of His body, of His one body, and always be thankful. It says that the anointed one, which is Jesus, will guide you with His peace. God does not exist in confusion and chaos. While the situation and circumstances and everything around you might not look right or be chaotic, you can be at peace when you follow God.

Remember, when you have the Holy Spirit and you're in a relationship with God, you're talking to God. What's going to happen is when a change is coming, much like Elijah, He will give you signs. You don't need to get all worried and chaotic. No. The minute it's time for you to move or change or switch into something else, He will tell you, 'Okay, now move.' You are actually following peace. Everything can be falling apart around you and you are completely and totally at peace. Why? Because God has not said "run around like a chicken with your head cut off". If you are already in that relationship where you're speaking to Him every day, you have a prayer life and you're reading the bible, when there's a change coming He's going to tell you there's a change.

I have a testimony to share with you. Years ago, within the first year of being saved, I was already talking to God; I already had a relationship with the Lord. He was speaking to me so I knew to follow what the Lord was doing and not be caught up in what was going on around me.

I did a lot of mission work. One mission trip I went on numerous times was to the island of Haiti. They had just had a natural disaster in that country and I felt led to host a fundraiser for them where we would collect all the proceeds and send it to a team that was working there. They have orphanages and they're taking care of over 1,000 kids and people there. I spoke to the church about it. I said, 'Let's put on a barbecue and the proceeds will go to Haiti.'

They said, 'Yes, that's a great idea. Let's do that.'

We were planning this barbecue six months out from the day it would take place. There was a whole committee and different people were in charge of different portions of the barbecue. My job in the whole thing was to get the food. They asked me how many people we should be preparing for, so I said, '500.' How did I come up with this number? I don't know. It felt like 500 to me so I said let's do for 500. Each person is getting their portion of responsibility together and we're meeting once per month. When it came down to the last month before the barbecue, we started to meet every week.

Two weeks before the date of the barbecue, we are having a meeting. I wasn't saved for a very long time, it was under a year. So to everyone I was a new believer. During the meeting, they're going around the table asking each person who is in charge of a portion how things are going.

'Do you have the bounce houses for the kids secured?'

'Yes, I have that' was the response.

'I have the music' and so forth.

They get to me and they asked, 'How's it going with the food?' It's 2 weeks before the event.

So I said, 'It's going. It will be okay.'

They ask, 'Well, what do you have so far to feed these 500 people?' By then they had already sold 497 tickets for this barbecue. People are coming.

I said, 'Oh, I don't have anything yet.' You should have seen look on their faces! And rightfully so. I'm telling you this story because you would probably have been shocked too. 2 weeks before the date and there is no food, nothing. I said, 'I don't have anything but it's going to be okay, we're going to be okay.' They are looking at me and asking if they should jump in and help.

I said, 'No, I got this. It's going to be fine.' I could tell they were in a panic. Just imagine, you sell tickets for a barbecue and there's no food, at 2 weeks out. I said, 'it's okay,' because quite frankly, I was at peace.

No, I'm not going to tell you or anyone else for that matter to do this. I can only go with the peace of God that was in my own heart, what I was feeling at that moment because the idea of the barbecue came from Him. All the ideas came from Him. I'm talking God. The amount of people we were supposed to have, that came from Him. So why wouldn't He give us the food?

We left the meeting but I could tell, and this is a large church that flows heavily in the spirit of excellence, they're not going to let some new believer ruin their reputation by not having the food portion covered. I could tell they were already, in their minds, probably saying that we have sold tickets for $10 or $15 a ticket, we can get hamburgers and hot dogs for that and still have money to donate.

But that wasn't my goal. My goal was to not pay for anything. We're going to get everything free, all donated so that all the money that comes in goes straight to the cause, not deduct money for food. That was how I got this from the Lord. But I knew they were probably thinking they would need to buy hamburgers and hot dogs at the last minute because I probably won't get it done. I could tell that was what they were thinking.

I left and went home, and I was at peace.

It was going to be fine. There was not going to be a problem. The following Monday we were scheduled to have our last meeting before the barbecue which was scheduled for Saturday.

On Tuesday, I go to work and I said to the Lord, 'So what are we going to do about the food for the barbecue?' It was my lunch break and I went online and I did a little Google search for barbecue. Up pops this place, it's like the biggest barbecue joint in the area. Everybody knows this place. They are well known for their barbecue. They have the best ribs, even though I'd never been there before because I wasn't much of a ribs person. But it was highly rated online so it just felt right. So I picked up my keys, got in my car and drove over there. When I got there, nothing was happening because apparently they don't open until about four in the afternoon and it's about 12:30pm. Nothing went on there in the mornings. I tried the front door and it was actually open! I walked in the door and there's this man standing out in the lobby. The place is called Bud's. I walk in and I said, 'Oh hi, are you Bud?'

The man says, 'Yah, I'm Bud.' I said, 'Bud, my name is Nicole and I'm doing a fundraiser for my church and we're having a barbecue to help the people of Haiti who just suffered that natural disaster several month ago. I was wondering if you could donate to us. Maybe some ribs, or chicken, whatever you can.' I said this to him and he is standing there like he is in shock with his mouth hanging open. I'm thinking, what did I say to him that's making him look like that.

He says to me, 'Did you read the Palm Beach Post this morning?'

I told him, 'No, I didn't read the paper.' He said to wait right there and he walked off to his office or in the back somewhere. He comes back with the newspaper and he opens it and there is this whole news spread in the center of the newspaper about the disaster in Haiti, about the people who were suffering, about everything that was happening. It came out that day. What are the chances that the same day that I walk into his restaurant there is a center spread on a story that happened 6 months ago? This wasn't a new story. It was an old story that just happened to coincide with my visit.

He then proceeded to tell me, 'I just read this five minutes ago. I finished reading it and I sat at my desk and I said to

God, 'God, I need to do something to help these people. Show me what I can do to help these people. I walk out of my office and I'm just standing here and you walk in the door.'

Can you believe that? He says, 'Yes, of course. What do you need?' I told him it was for 500 people. He told me to come back Saturday morning at this time and he'll give me ribs and chicken for the 500 people.

I will tell you, I did not have a letter from the church, nothing. I just walked straight in and started talking.

I said 'Thank you' and turned around and got back in my car. I went back to the office.

Wednesday rolls around, and I said to myself, 'What else do we need for the barbecue? We have ribs and we have chicken. It would be nice to have some fried chicken, hamburgers, and hot dogs. We'll need condiments and things. So I go back online. I search again for another place. Church's chicken is fried chicken.

Okay, cool. Then there are supermarkets too, right, Winn Dixie and Publix. I get into my car and I drive over to Church's chicken. I said the same thing the manager. The manager tells me, 'I'm going to give you 250 pieces of fried chicken.

On the way back, I see Winn Dixie. I pulled in and asked for the manager. I said I wanted 500 hamburgers and hot dogs.

By Tuesday and Wednesday, I had all the food. Everything, barbecued ribs, barbecued chicken, fried chicken, hamburgers, hot dogs, and all the condiments and all the drinks. In 2 days! With no letter, just some person that walked in off the street.

I was at peace because I followed the peace of God. That's what led me. I'm not going to get all worked up. It was His idea, so He has to provide for it. It was His idea, not mine.

Of course the following Monday, I go to the meeting and I sit there and they ask me first, because you know they are worried. I tell them what happened. Now they are all looking at me with the same look that Bud had, shocked.

The church administrator says to me, 'So, you met Bud?'

I answered, 'Yeah, he was standing in the lobby.'

The administrator says, 'That place has been there for nearly 20 years and no one has ever met Bud. We even started wondering if he existed. No one has ever met him.'

Then I told him 'Well, I met him; Bud was in the lobby and had just happened to read the story on Tuesday morning in the Palm Beach Post.'

Another person commented that large supermarket chains generally don't give away that much food on a local level that those decisions are generally made at the corporate office. I told them on Wednesday they both did it with no hesitation and without directing me to the corporate office.

So this isn't just about peace, this is also about the timing of God. If I had run out there before Tuesday, there would have been no newspapers article for him to read and say yes to or say a prayer to God and God send me into his lobby 5 minutes later. I didn't even know he was a believer in Christ until he told me that.

This is why you have to follow the peace of God, because the peace of God is also attached to the timing of God which will move you into something in the right time, in the right season and put you in the right place. You can't follow what's going on around you in terms of news, media, and social media. No. You read the bible, you pray God will tell you and you follow the peace of God and you don't allow outside forces to influence your thinking.

If God has said to you, 'I got it; I'm going to take care of this for you.' Trust Him.

Near the end of the meeting someone commented that it had been raining so hard and would be raining for the entire week, including Saturday.

I chimed in and told them "No, it's not going to rain on Saturday". When I said that you could hear a pin drop.

They went dead silent turned and looked at me and someone said to me sarcastically, "so, you can control the weather now too?"

I said "no, but why would God have us put on this barbecue, confirm that He's behind all of this by causing us to sell all these tickets, get everything completely donated and take us right into the day of the event just to make it rain?" That doesn't make any sense. Truly, sometimes it's just common sense. And sure enough, it rained for 2 weeks straight except on the Saturday of the barbecue. No rain. Then it picked right up and started raining again on Sunday.

The next way God speaks to us is through His creation.

Psalm 19:1-4 'The heavens declare the glory of God; the skies proclaim the work of His hands. Day after day they pour forth speech. Night after night they reveal knowledge. There is no speech nor language Where their voice is not heard. Their line has gone out through all the earth, And their words to the end of the world.'

Isn't it interesting that all of God's creation knows what God is doing. Birds know when it's time to migrate and what to do. It's all in the environment, it's in creation. The creation that is outside tells you, if you just pay attention to it.

We know there is a change when the leaves change color and fall off. Then it snows. Then there is spring. The environment around us speaks of changes in seasons. The animals know it, the plants know it and as humans we can pick up on what God is doing if we in turn look at His creation.

You know I have often thought how will the entire world be evangelized? How are they all going to know that God exists if we don't tell them?

Romans 1:20 "For since the creation of the world His invisible attributes are clearly seen, being understood by the things that are made, even His eternal power and Godhead, so that they are without excuse,"

Here God says it clearly that He will speak through creation. There is no way you can look at the world around you and believe there is no God. None of us will have an excuse.

***

Personal Reflections:

Have you ever invited God to reveal Himself to you through your senses?

Using the list of senses below, describe an instance when it's possible God was talking to you.

Sight

Sound

Smell

Taste

Touch

***

Prayer:

Holy Spirit,

I am asking You now to activate my spiritual senses so that I will be able to see, hear, smell, taste and feel the Presence and Voice of God. I thank You that in asking, seeking and knocking this door will be opened to me. I thank You that I will be able to hear God speak clearly and not only once but every single day. Thank You for leaving us the gift of the bible as a starting point to accessing Your voice, in Jesus name,

Amen

***

Chapter 3

Stewarding And Growing In The Voice Of God

Stewardship. What is stewardship?

*I*t comes from the Greek word 'oikonomeó'. It means the manager of a household, the household manager, a steward or guardian to whom the head of the house or proprietor has entrusted the management of his affairs, to care for receipts and expenditures, and the duty of dealing out the proper portion to every servant, or even to the children not yet of age.

That's interesting, isn't it? You're giving to those who are not yet of age, you're stewarding, you are managing what God has given you. This is stewardship.

Then the question is, 'How would you properly steward the voice of God?' You properly steward the voice of God by properly managing how He is speaking to you.

You already know that He is speaking through our five senses and His voice is multifaceted coming through different forums; dreams and visions, through the bible, through the situational changes, through nature, through many other ways.

So, how would stewardship look? Let's say you're a dreamer and you have dreams. To properly steward your dreams would mean when you get them, as soon as you wake up in the morning or even in the middle of the night if you keep a voice recorder at the side of your bed, you record what the dream was about, you record what time you woke up, what the dream was, if there was any scripture that you received in the dream, or any impression of a scripture that came to you. You would record how you felt, your emotional state. You're going to record the colors, any smells, anything that are associated with that dream, you're going to write it all down.

Why is this important? If you don't write it down, you're going to forget. You won't be able to steward something you don't remember. Have you ever tried going to a supermarket without a list, even if you only need four items? The minute you're in there you're like; 'I have three, what's the fourth one? I don't remember.' Then you get all the way back home and that's when you remember and what's worse is sometimes it's one of the main ingredients so you have to go back to the store.

Well, the same thing is going to happen when God says something to you, if you don't write it down, you're going to forget what He said and then you'll have no reference, no dates of when He said something or what He said.

Stewarding is really just record keeping so that you can put action to what you wrote or recorded.

As things happen or you see the fruition of the dream, you will be able to go back into your journal and check to see what dream you had, on what date, what God said about it and how it manifested itself. You have a full record of everything from start to finish. When you start doing this, you may begin to pick up on a pattern in which God speaks to you personally, it's your individual language with God, so to speak.

It is so important that if it is the voice of God, He's speaking to your spirit, you need to write that down as well and you need to write down what happened when you did what He told you to do. What were the results? What was the fruit of it? God can trust that you have a record of what He told you to do so you have something that you can go back to, and you're not just trying to remember.

I want to share a story with you of how God was working with me, in moving me from one way of speaking or hearing His voice to another. In case this happens to you, you'll understand what is going on and probably handle it a little better than I did.

When I had just gotten saved, His way of speaking with me was really two main ways; through the word directly as I read the bible, the scriptures would come to me and I would record them and I would know what to do from that. I would step out and do whatever it is He was saying to do.

Then He would speak directly into my spirit. Different people feel their spirit man in other areas but I can tell you with one hundred percent certainty mine was not audibly and it wasn't in my mind. It was somewhere inside of me. I heard the voice of God and He would just talk to me straight. When you have that, it's very easy to know what to do because there's no misinterpretation of the information. It's just, 'He said this and I did it.' There was no questioning; did He mean this or did He mean that. It makes being obedient that much easier because the message is clear.

What you're going to find as you begin to do what the Lord tells you to do, is you're going to start growing.

At exactly my one year spiritual birthday, He stopped speaking into my spirit and He switched into dreams. I didn't like that very much because, if you get dreams you know what I'm talking about, it's all these symbols and none of it makes sense and what does this mean and what does that mean plus I wasn't writing anything down. Nobody told me to record or write down what the Lord was telling me. Nobody did, so I wasn't doing that at all.

I would get them like every other night, it was so complicated and I would just ignore them and move on because I was waiting for Him to talk to me in my spirit like He always did. Except, He didn't.

As time started to go on for about a couple weeks, I asked myself what was going on, why wasn't God talking to me, in my spirit. I started thinking I must have done something wrong. I wondered what I had done to make God mad at me because God was not talking to me anymore. I thought I did something wrong so I asked Him, 'Well, why aren't You talking to me anymore?' One of the ways I knew I hadn't really done anything wrong was my prayers were still getting answered and things were flowing as normal. He was just not speaking into my spirit anymore. I was having all these dreams and I really didn't like it because I didn't know what to do with the symbols.

Where do I go for this? You know who I'm going to ask about this. I didn't understand so I kind of just pushed it off, I didn't want anything to do with the dreams. I just ignored it. Well, God doesn't care if you want to learn that or not. If He says this is what we're doing this season, this is how I'm talking to you; you need to get on board with it. He's not conforming to us, we are the ones that need to conform to Him.

Let's say you live in London, England and you speak English you'll be able to understand everyone around you. Then He picks you up and He drops you over in Germany. He says, 'here, now speak German.' NO! Take me back to England, I don't want to do this, I don't like this. But no, I have to learn it because now we're at another level and in a different country.

I took my time. I bought books. I started reading about dream language, how to interpret dreams, learning what smells mean, what do colors mean, what does this mean, and what does that mean.

This is not really about dreams per se. This is about a change in the way in which He speaks because He will do that. For you it could be something else, but the key is to recognize when the channel that He is using to communicate has changed. How else are you going to grow if He doesn't switch the language or the way in which He communicates? Once I learned, and believe me it takes a while, this opened the door for many other ways in which He began to speak to me because now I get visions. Now I can walk out and look at things and pick up messages just from understanding dream symbols, whereas before that would mean nothing to me.

I'm telling you this to let you know that He will move you into a different type of language and way in which He speaks when He's pushing you to grow.

Think of it like a house. You have different ways in which you access a house. There is your front door, depending on the house, you have a garage door, and you have a side door to get into the garage. Further around the house you have a door that goes into the kitchen. You might have a side pool screen door and another screen door on that side. Then there is a door to get into the back door. There are several doors to get into a house. Usually the voice of God is like that. He's not going to give you just one way to hear Him. He's going to grow you in each of these ways so that you can access Him and He can speak to you through many different ways.

The main way I started was with the bible. So the bible is your front door. But then He's going to move you into something else. Maybe your next thing will be having Him speak into your spirit. That's your garage door. Then you come around to the side and now we're going into dreams. Dreams are your kitchen door. Now we're in the back, in the pool area and visions come into play.

Why would He do this? What if someone or something is barring you from entering the front door? You have many other ways you can access the house so you don't need to worry that your communication is being cut off.

He wants to make sure that you can access that house through many different ways not just one door.

A friend of mine has her main way of speaking and hearing from God through the bible. A number of years ago I told her she really needed to start speaking in tongues more. She is not from a church that teaches or believes this so she was a little hesitant. I said, 'I know. I'm telling you, you need to grow in that some more. Just do it because wisdom will come to you through that and you'll start to hear God in many different ways through speaking in tongues. She started with that and sure enough, within several months she had to have eye surgery and she wasn't be able to read her bible because she didn't have her vision. That's her front door. Even after the surgery, it took quite a while before her vision came back. It was blurry. If she hadn't had another way to hear from God, she would have been incapacitated for months, sitting there feeling like she couldn't hear anything because she was not reading.

Do not fight when God begins to move His voice into another place. Embrace it. He's just training you in another way to hear from Him and you need to embrace that.

I want to share this scripture with you. This is one of those scriptures that the first time I read it, I didn't get it. It didn't sound Christian to me even though it was in the bible. I just didn't understand it.

Matthew 25:14-29 The Parable of the talents.'For the kingdom of heaven is like a man traveling to a far country, who called his own servants and delivered his goods to them. And to one he gave five talents, to another two, and to another one, to each according to his own ability; and immediately he went on a journey. Then he who had received the five talents went and traded with them, and made another five talents. And likewise he who had received two gained two more also. But he who had received one went and dug in the ground, and hid his lord's money. After a long time the lord of those servants came and settled accounts with them.

"So he who had received five talents came and brought five other talents, saying, 'Lord, you delivered to me five talents; look, I have gained five more talents besides them.' His lord said to him, 'Well done, good and faithful servant; you were faithful over a few things,

I will make you ruler over many things. Enter into the joy of your lord.' He also who had received two talents came and said, 'Lord, you delivered to me two talents; look, I have gained two more talents besides them.' His lord said to him, 'Well done, good and faithful servant; you have been faithful over a few things, I will make you ruler over many things. Enter into the joy of your lord.'

"Then he who had received the one talent came and said, 'Lord, I knew you to be a hard man, reaping where you have not sown, and gathering where you have not scattered seed. And I was afraid, and went and hid your talent in the ground. Look, there you have what is yours.'

"But his lord answered and said to him, 'You wicked and lazy servant, you knew that I reap where I have not sown, and gather where I have not scattered seed. So you ought to have deposited my money with the bankers, and at my coming I would have received back my own with interest. So take the talent from him, and give it to him who has ten talents.

'For to everyone who has, more will be given, and he will have abundance; but from him who does not have, even what he has will be taken away. '

Isn't that interesting? Let's look at that last part again.

'For to everyone who has will be given more and he will have abundance.' So if you have more, He's going to give you more on top of that to abundance. But then to the one who doesn't have anything, He takes it away.

The first time I read that I thought it was a little harsh. I thought you would want to give to the one with less, right? I didn't understand it.

I'm going to use this as how you grow in hearing the voice of God because you are stewarding. Remember it says the master left and he gave them things to watch over, steward over. God starts speaking to you through the bible. You heard from the Lord, what are you going to do with it? You have something valuable in your hands, it's valuable. You have to go and produce with that.

God says, 'I'm going to show you this. I'm revealing this to you.'

You say, 'Lord, what do you want me to do with this?' He says you need to pray over it. So you pray and then you see the fruit of that in someone else's life. You are taking what He is saying to you and you are producing something good from it as opposed to you doing nothing with what you heard Him tell you to do. This would be one scenario.

The other scenario is that He gives you a scripture and you read it and you are packing in all this knowledge, you know this and you know that.

But what did you do with that? Nothing. You sit there getting fat on the word and you haven't done anything, no actions. There's no fruit coming off it. Nothing is being produced from it. He's talking to you through His word and you're not doing anything with it, just taking it all in. Do you think God will come and say anything else to you when you haven't done anything with the last thing He told you?

Let's look at another person. God says in His word, 'Listen, I'm going to show you something. You see this over there?' And that person responds, 'Wow, God! This is a great cause. I need to support this.' And He says, 'Yes. Go and financially support them.' The person goes ahead and does what God told them to do.

Now that person, who is growing in the word of God through obeying the voice of God in His word, is going to be given another gift on top of that because God says he did such a good job managing His word. Here comes another gift! I'm going to start talking to you through your spirit. You start to hear through your spirit and you go off and do what He tells you. God can trust you because you're doing what He's telling you to do. Now you are learning and listening to Him that way. God says He's going to add another one on to you. Then He says He is going to give you a fifth way now, and then a sixth way, and then He's going to add a seventh way because you are stewarding that so well. You are producing fruit with what He is saying. You're not just taking it for yourself and not doing anything with it. That is stewarding in God's voice and growing in God's voice.

As you steward it, you have to action it. He loves to talk to us but there has to be some fruit. God is not just going to sit around and gossip with you about other people. There is a reason why He's showing you certain things.

Whether it's in your world, it's in your church, or it's in the economy, you have to do something with it. The first call is generally prayer. Pray about it. You'll see changes happening as a result of your prayer because you've taken that and you did something with it. You'll say I support this or He'll say go over there and tell this person that or I need you to do this with it. You have to do something when He speaks. That's how you manage the talents now growing.

All of these are things that you have to do for yourself. You have to take what I'm sharing with you and action it. You have to go and do the exercises. You're the one who has to spend time with the Lord and you're the one who has to go in a relationship with the Lord. I can't actually give that to you. No matter how much I pray for you, it doesn't happen until you do it.

There is a saying that goes like this. Prayer is caught, not taught. There are some books you can read and they can be so well written, but did it inspire you to pray? No, because it's just words on a page until you actually open your mouth and do it and see the power of it. Then you start to catch on to it because you're engaging it.

Here is another parable that demonstrates this.

Matthew 25:1-12 "Then the kingdom of heaven shall be likened to ten virgins who took their lamps and went out to meet the bridegroom. Now five of them were wise, and five were foolish. Those who were foolish took their lamps and took no oil with them, ⁴ but the wise took oil in their vessels with their lamps. But while the bridegroom was delayed, they all slumbered and slept.

"And at midnight a cry was heard: 'Behold, the bridegroom ⌐is coming; go out to meet him!' Then all those virgins arose and trimmed their lamps. And the foolish said to the wise, 'Give us some of your oil, for our lamps are going out.' But the wise answered, saying, 'No, lest there should not be enough for us and you; but go rather to those who sell, and buy for yourselves.' And while they went to buy, the bridegroom came, and those who were ready went in with him to the wedding; and the door was shut.

"Afterward the other virgins came also, saying, 'Lord, Lord, open to us!' But he answered and said, 'Assuredly, I say to you, I do not know you.'

Both groups are waiting for the Lord. He shows up, half of them have oil and the other half don't. The ones that don't have oil ask for a loan, give us some of your oil. The ones with oil tell them to go get their own because they don't want to run out as well. When I read this as a new Christian, I was trying to figure out why they couldn't just give them some of their oil. But this parable is talking about that intimate relationship with the Lord. I can't give you mine. I can't give you my relationship with the Lord.

Have you ever looked at a couple who seem to have an amazing marriage and say to yourself, 'I wish I had a marriage like that?' Well, those people had to work at that, he had to invest and she had to invest and that is why their marriage looks the way it does.

It takes time and energy and each person has to be intentional. The relationship didn't get that way by accident.

If the husband does his own thing and the wife does her own thing, they're not spending time together, how is that marriage going to work? It won't. Each person has to invest in it to get out of it what they want, the good result.

We are the Bride of Christ. He is our Bridegroom. Our relationship requires time and we have to be intentional about it.

Here's an analogy for you. We all have the same 24 hours in a day. We do not have any less time than Moses had or Abraham had or Joshua, or any of those people. It's the same time. But what happens is our world right now compared to theirs is so crammed with voices, with social media, with TV, with the internet, with these constant messages everywhere. There is so much vying for our attention. We have to get to the point where we shut it down. There are just too many voices, too much noise.

Imagine you and your co-worker are at work. The boss tells you tomorrow morning he is going to do something very special with all of you. He says to make sure you show up on time so you don't miss out on anything. 'We're going to go some place and I have something really special to show you.'

Now imagine you need gas in your car and you decide you'll stop on the way home to get gas so that you will have that out of the way. It's like the oil thing. On your way home that evening, you stop and get gas so that you have a full tank for tomorrow because you need to be prepared for this meeting. You make sure you make it on time. You understand how important the meeting is tomorrow so you don't want to wait until the last minute; you want to take care of it the evening before.

Your co-worker has a quarter tank of gas. They also decide to get gas in the evening before going home. But they are on the phone talking, picking up the kids from school, they have to get dinner, they have to do this and that. They say they will get gas after this phone call. But after this call is another. They plan to get gas after they pick up the kids but then they forget and the next thing they know, they are home. They don't want to go out again; their shows are on the TV. They say they will get gas in the morning on the way to work.

You already have a full tank of gas and you are now home. You go to sleep and get up and go directly to work. You're heading out now and so is your co-worker, who happens to be running late. They have to drop off the kids and then get gas. But they forget and get on the highway. Now their gas gauge is almost on empty. They were so busy, they forgot to get gas. Now there is an accident and you are both stuck in traffic. So neither one of you is ahead of the other. You are both stuck in traffic. You are both in the same boat, the only difference is one of you is on empty and the other is not. Your co-worker's car is stuck in traffic so long on empty, and it gets to the point where the car shuts off. Now the traffic starts to move and as you are driving by very slowly and your co-worker yells out to you that they need gas because they don't have any and they ask you to give them some of yours. How exactly are you supposed to do that? You're going to say you can't get out of line; you need to get to work for that big meeting today with the boss. You can't be late. You tell them to call a tow truck company to come and help them. That's all you can do, really.

Think of it that way. You cannot help someone with an intimate relationship with the Lord. They have to cultivate their own. Some things you can't lend or borrow from someone else. It doesn't matter how much you pray for your kids to come to know the Lord or you teach them about Christ, they have to learn to develop that as they get older. That fire has to spark inside of them where they begin to hunger for God as much as you do because you cannot impart that.

This is how you grow in hearing the Voice of God. We all have the same number of hours in the day. You just have to make it a priority to spend time with Jesus.

You will grow leaps and bounds as you do this.

***

Personal Reflection:

Stewardship begins with writing things down or recording it on a device.

Start by just listing the important information so you can return when you have more time or are wide awake to create a narrative with many more details. The basics should trigger memories.

Leave some space so you can return to the entry and add notes or outcomes, maybe using a different color ink.

Begin small. Take baby steps. A daily planner may be a good way to start. Write SOMETHING every day. As you become accustomed to the process, you will develop skills so your entries will also develop.

***

Prayer:

Abba Father,

I cherish Your voice more than anything else in the world. Thank You for taking the time to meet with me and speak to me daily. I ask that You give me a diligent spirit to steward everything You say to me in a manner that is pleasing to You. Help me to grow in all the areas of hearing Your voice, in Jesus name.

Amen.

***

Chapter 4

Five Things That Will Affect How You Hear From God

*T*here are five things that will affect how you are hearing God's voice in your life. These are really important because sometimes we can hear things and wonder if it is God or is it not God. When we are mindful of these things it will be easier for us to pick up on whether it is God or something else. They will also help affect how you hear what you hear because sometimes we can hear things and think it's God when really it's not and it has to do with the source, where the information came from.

Every message that comes to us has three possible sources; God's voice, the enemy's voice, or it's our own personal voice.

What I'm going to share with you is going to limit the other two sources from getting through so you will be able to better discern, decipher or hone in on God's voice and what God is saying.

The first thing that will affect how you hear God is when you don't *renew* of your heart, your mind, your soul, and your strength.

Matthew 22:37 "Jesus said to him, "'You shall love the Lord your God with all your heart, with all your soul, and with all your mind.'"

This bible tells us that we renew our mind by offering our bodies as a living sacrifice to God. Then He will show us what is pleasing and acceptable to His will.

Romans 12:1-2"I beseech you therefore, brethren, by the mercies of God, that you present your bodies a living sacrifice, holy, acceptable to God, which is your reasonable service. And do not be conformed to this world, but be transformed by the renewing of your mind, that you may prove what is that good and acceptable and perfect will of God."

We renew our mind by reading the word of God so that our mind becomes filled with God's word so that when we hear something, we know whether it is God or not. From a renewed mind we begin the process of what's going on in our soul and in our physical bodies. What we lust for or desire will make it difficult for us to hear God if these things are not renewed and regenerated in His word and by His truth. We are not following what society says, what the media says, what the culture is saying or anything else around us, we're following what God's word is saying to us.

This is our Truth.

By renewing these parts of us, we will then be able to discern God's voice and we can only renew through the word of God. The word of God is the only authority we will use to discern God's voice. This is how you test everything.

1 John 4:1a"Beloved, do not believe every spirit, but test the spirits, whether they are of God;"

The second thing that will affect how you hear God is when you don't *settle* our issues with the word. What does that mean; settle your issue? When you become a believer in Christ and you start reading the bible. You're going to have some things that you read that are really going to go against what you believe. If you've been believing your entire life what is in the media or what some celebrity said, or what you heard from this person or that, and you held onto those things as truths, when you come across a scripture in the bible that completely refutes all of that, it will challenge your belief system. That creates an issue; you now have an issue with a particular principle or scripture in the bible that needs to be settled.

What will happen if you don't address this, is if God is trying to get your attention or talk to you about something that is opposing what you know as truth, you won't want to hear it because you've already accepted that other thing as truth.

Settling the issue means you need to remove that from your mind as truth and replace it with what the word of God says. I can assure you this is not as easy as it sounds.

John 17:17 "Sanctify them by Your truth. Your word is truth"

For years you believed this, but now you've decided to no longer hold onto that as truth because now you know that the truth is God's word. There is no other Truth.

I'm going to give you an example of how I had to settle my issue with the word on two separate issues.

When I got saved and I was reading the bible, there were really two things that I came across in the word of God that I just didn't know if I believed them. I'm being honest with you so that when it happens to you, I want you to be able to identify it.

One of them was fornication. Fornication is having sex out of the context of marriage. If you are married and you have an affair with someone, that's adultery. I wasn't in a relationship with anyone at the time, so thank God I didn't have to get rid of anyone. But I had a problem with this in the bible. How can it be true?

Society has said for so long that it is okay. I was just fighting this because this is a need, isn't it? I didn't understand what the big deal was because in society, we work around it *even* as Christians. We think, 'I'm engaged.' or 'I already have children with this person' and we find all kinds of excuses to justify what we're doing. The bible clearly says it's not okay. When I read the bible and came across it and I studied it out and I knew what it was, it was one of those things that I had to put up on a shelf. I had a mental block against it.

I decided I would have to come back to it, skip that one for now and we'll circle back on it later.

I was 30 years old at that time and I wasn't in a relationship, but that meant that if I didn't get married, I was going to have to live the rest of my life without …that. Well, I didn't sign up to be a nun! I had a problem with it. At that time, I didn't want to get married so that means this issue was never going to be resolved. So I take it, put it up on a shelf, and leave it there.

The other thing I had an issue with involved my circle of friends. At one point in my life, all my male friends were gay, all of them, every single one. We would all hang out and go everywhere together. I am not gay but I sure did have a lot of friends who were. I still do.

To read in the word of God where it says that is a sin and, of course, I had an instant issue with this one. I have friends and I love my friends, we have been friends for years. So how am I supposed to deal with this one? What am I going to say to them? I had a problem with this, so up on the shelf it went because I couldn't accept it. I needed to find in the bible the 'workaround'. How do I get out of this? There must be a door in the scriptures that says, 'Aha' this used to be a thing but today you can just ignore it! I was searching for this scripture and couldn't seem to find it.

I'm going along and the months are rolling by, I'm following God's word, I do everything the Lord tells me to do and as I started to see answered prayer and how God was talking to me through the bible and as I followed what the Lord was saying, my life was flourishing and getting better and better and better.

I started to realize this bible is the truth. Everything it says to do, when you do it, it works. These are principles for living daily life, it works. I got to the point where I had read the entire bible and I did what it said, I obeyed. I saw it working.

I got to the point where I told myself if all of this is true, why do I have these two things up on my shelf? I had to face those issues. I can't take part of the bible and not the rest of it when all the parts that I am applying to my life work. Why would everything in it be true except for these two things?

It means all of it has to be true. I had to sit with the Lord and talk to Him about my friends. Yes, homosexuals generally feel that Christians judge them secretly and hate them. I still remember the look of terror on their faces when I told them I became a Christian. It was like they were expecting me to turn into a different person and start saying hateful things to them. I didn't do that.

When I spoke with the Lord about this He said He never told any of us to hate anybody, He isn't telling me to hit anyone over the head with the bible, He isn't telling me to love them any less than I loved them before I found out this Truth. He said they were still His children and He still loves them no matter what. You can still treat them with love and respect and kindness. I just needed to know what His word says. I need to acknowledge His Truth. So if I ever get asked, I have to respond with His Truth, in love. I cannot deny the Truth but I need to be loving in how I deliver the Truth when asked.

On that day, I settled my issue and took these two things off the shelf and decided to agree with this Truth and accept His Truth. Not just the parts I'm okay with, all of it.

Once I decided to accept it as truth, everything was cleared. It wasn't this issue first and then that issue followed. No.

This is when I realized something really key. Everything comes from a root. The root of the two issues I'm telling you about is called sexual immorality. That's the root. I had a tree and the root of the tree is sexual immorality. Out of sexual immorality comes the fruit of it which will manifest differently with different people. So I really had an issue with sexual immorality and once that got resolved the two fruit that were manifesting in my life got removed. Out of sexual immorality comes many things like adultery, fornication, pornography, masturbation, lust, etc. They are actually attached to the one root. I realized what happened that day is God delivered me from that, He took that root out and anything that was attached to it is gone.

The point is He was not able to speak to me on anything regarding any of these subjects until I settled the issue. And it's going to be the same with you if you have an issue with anything in the word that you're reading. You will never be able to hear God clearly on that because you've basically taken you own opinion, your own idea, what you heard in the world, what you saw in the media, what you got from your friends and you put it above the word of God.

And that's never going to work!

When He starts talking to you, you can't hear it because you don't believe what you are hearing and it's going to affect how you hear God.

If you give the enemy a toe hold he'll take a foot hold and when he takes a foot hold he goes in for a strong hold next. If I didn't settle these issues, the two would've turned into three and then three turns into four and so on and so forth. Eventually I would've started questioning many things about God's word.

The third thing that will affect how you hear God is *syncretism*. This is the union or attempted fusion of different systems of thought or belief, especially in religion or philosophy.

It's taking two things that shouldn't go together and it's fusing them into one. We see this over and over again in the Old Testament. God gave His people a command of driving out all the false idol worshipping but they would only do a part of the instructions and not the rest of it. This ultimately led to their downfall.

Numbers 33:51-5 "Speak to the children of Israel, and say to them: 'When you have crossed the Jordan into the land of Canaan, then you shall drive out all the inhabitants of the land from before you, destroy all their engraved stones, destroy all their molded images, and demolish all their high places; you shall dispossess the inhabitants of the land and dwell in it, for I have given you the land to possess."

2 Kings 17:7-12, 16-18"...the children of Israel secretly did against the Lord their God things that were not right, and they built for themselves high places in all their cities, from watchtower to fortified city. They set up for themselves sacred pillars and wooden images on every high hill and under every green tree. ¹There they burned incense on all the high places, like the nations whom the Lord had carried away before them; and they did wicked things to provoke the Lord to anger, for they served idols, of which the Lord had said to them, "You shall not do this thing."

So they left all the commandments of the Lord their God, made for themselves a molded image and two calves, made a wooden image and worshiped all the host of heaven, and served Baal. And they caused their sons and daughters to pass through the fire, practiced witchcraft and soothsaying, and sold themselves to do evil in the sight of the Lord, to provoke Him to anger. Therefore the Lord was very angry with Israel, and removed them from His sight; there was none left but the tribe of Judah alone."

God will say to them, 'I need you to go in and I need you to remove these idols and get rid of this and then the bible will say they removed this, this, and that but they kept this. The next person, child or son who comes in may have a downfall because of the one thing they didn't get rid of.

I would read these stories and think, 'I don't understand. What are they not getting? They saw that their father fell because of this. Why didn't they just stop doing it?'

I couldn't understand that because in my head that was back then. They were involved in idolatry. They were doing this, and that is why they failed. It's easy to think this is some Old Testament concept that doesn't happen today.

Deuteronomy 7:5 'but thus shall ye deal with them. You shall destroy their altars, break down their images, cut down their groves, and burn their graven images with fire.'

2 Chronicles 14: 2-7 'Asa, which is one of the kings, did what was good and right in the eyes of the Lord his God. He removed the altars of the foreign gods and the high places, broke down the sacred pillars, cut down the wooden images. He commanded Judah to seek the Lord their God, the God of their fathers and to observe the law and the commandments. He also removed the high places and the incense altars from all the cities of Judah and the kingdom was quiet under him. And he built the fortified cities in Judah and the land had rest and he had no wars for those years because the Lord had given him rest.'

He said to Judah. Let us build these cities and make walls around them, towers, gates, and bars while the land is yet before us because we have sought the Lord our God. We have sought Him and He has given us rest on every side. "

So they built and prospered. We see that Asa removed everything and he prospered. But as you go through Kings and the Chronicles, you're going to notice there were many that didn't remove all these false practices and as a result they failed. What does that look like today?

We read the bible, we say we are Christians but then we turn around and we're reading horoscopes.

We read the bible, we say we are Christians but then we go down to the strip mall on the corner and we talk to a psychic.

We read the bible, we say we are Christians then we go to palm readers reading our palms.

We read the bible, we say we are Christians but then we start to pick up these little practices from our mother, or grandmother, or maybe our great-grandmother. That's not Christian.

Well, what are some of these things, these practices?

Years ago, I went back to Jamaica, and a friend of my mother's bought land and was building a house and she asked if I would come over and say a prayer of blessings over the land. I agreed to come by and do that for her.

She told me she wants me to come on a particular day because the night before she was having a feast. She said she was going to save some goat blood so I could sprinkle it at the four corners of the house before I prayed. I asked why she would want to do that. Her response is that everybody did that. That was how everybody blessed their home.

I can say with certainty my family doesn't do this but she made me realize then that many other people do this. She was going to do something because everybody was doing it. She's not a bad person and in her mind she's not involved in witchcraft. No. She was doing it because everybody else did it that way.

I sat her down and explained to her, we don't do that. That isn't Christianity. We're not sprinkling any blood from animals around our house as Christians. I prayed over her land and blessed her house in the name of the Lord and that was all.

It does not matter how many people you see doing something, the day you come to know the Lord you have to begin examining all these cultural practices against the word of God.

When somebody dies, a few days before the actual funeral, they have something called the 'nine night'. They put out a plate of food so that the spirit of that person can have a final meal. All that happens in this transaction is they are calling demons into their house.

2 Corinthians 5:8 "We are confident, yes, well pleased rather to be absent from the body and to be present with the Lord."

When someone dies, they go straight to the Lord, if they are saved. I'm pretty sure heaven has much better food, with no calories! Therefore, they won't be coming to eat the food. Something is going to show up at your house but it won't be your loved one.

It's not Christian. But many Christians continue doing this because everybody else does it and it's a part of their culture. It's things like this that we do as Christians that is exactly like what the Israelites were doing and God told them to stop it.

Here is another very famous practice. People selling their house. What do they do? Have you heard about this Saint Joseph's statue? Yes, it's an actual statue. Christians and Catholics go online and buy one. It comes with prayers. This is Catholicism. You take the statue and dig a hole in the front of your yard. You turn the statue upside down and push it into the ground and cover it up. Then you pray this prayer over it that goes something like this.

I'm sorry I turned you on your head and I'm making you suffer, like Jesus suffered and I will take you out of your pain or your suffering after my house gets sold. Sell my house.

Now in addition to that prayer they are praying over the statue, there is a novena that they pray for seven or eight days following the burial of the statue that is an actual prayer to God to bless them.

Imagine the house gets sold, who is getting the credit for it? Is it the statue or is it the seven days of prayer that you actually prayed to God. So now all their faith is in the statue. If the house sold, they are automatically going to believe it was the statue, now they have implemented into their life some image or idol.

God doesn't get His glory and His credit, the statue is getting it. That is syncretism and once we start doing things like that, it starts to creep into other areas of our life.

We want to get rid of evil spirits so we going to burn sage. What other religion is that coming from? How is that going to help? It doesn't. You pray them out, that's how you get rid of evil spirits, by the power and the blood of Jesus.

We don't do syncretism or any other Jesus Christ plus system. No, we do straight Jesus. We read straight bible. We don't need any special oil, we don't need to throw salts, and we don't need to do any of that. God doesn't want that because what happens is we begin to put our trust in things that are not biblical, it's not God. We won't be able to hear the Lord when He's speaking to us.

I do a lot of mission work in Haiti. The statistics say that 56.8% of the people are Catholics, 29.6% are Protestants, and the rest are unaffiliated. However, 80% practice voodoo.

I've seen this myself while running medical clinics on our mission trips. Part of my job when I'm there is to share the gospel of Jesus Christ and bring them to the Lord. I hear over and over again, 'Oh I go to church but I found out that so-and-so was doing this to me so I had to go to this witch doctor to send a curse on them". They were coming from church and they go straight to the witch doctor.

One woman said she couldn't recommit or rededicate her life to Christ because she had already sold her soul to the devil. But she still goes to church on Sunday. If you ask if she was a

Christian, she would say yes. This is syncretism. It's Jesus plus something else.

This is a 2018 Pew Research study conducted in the United States of America. It says 40% of Christians believe in psychics, 38% Protestants, 46% Catholics, 33% Evangelicals. 26% of Christians believe in astrology, the horoscope, 34% Protestant, 33% Catholics. It says they believe but it doesn't say if they actually go. I have met and spoken with many people that still do both things.

There is a difference between astronomy and astrology. Astronomy is the science that studies everything outside of the earth's atmosphere such as stars, planets, asteroids, galaxies, the properties and relations of those celestial bodies.

The Jewish calendar is actually a lunar calendar and it works around the moon. If you think back to the Old Testament days, they didn't have calendars to tell them it was Sh'vat, Adar or Nisan (January, February, or March). They knew the seasons and when they changed by the moon. They're still using that today as their dates and their calendars. That is astronomy.

It was the star that led the Magis to Jesus. Astronomy.

Astrology, on the other hand, is the belief that the positioning of the stars and the planets are affecting what is going on in the earth. When you are reading your horoscope, somebody is saying to you this is going to happen to you because Venus is in Mars and Mercury is in retrograde or whatever it is they are saying, then they are letting you know that the sun and moon positioning is dictating your life. It is not Jesus. It is not God.

You shouldn't be thinking you can't marry or be friends with someone because of their "sign". When we are regenerated by reading God's word the only thing that identifies us is that we are children of God. We shouldn't look or act like an astrological sign, we should look like Him.

Therefore, these things don't matter and should have no bearing on our decisions. This will only compete with God's voice in our lives and this is the reason we should have nothing to do with it.

The fourth way that will affect how you hear God is thinking that it is an *event* that happens in a specific place. That means sometimes we might think we should go to church on Sunday from 9:00-10:30 and that's where I go to hear God. Inside the church building. I should go to this woman's conference because when I go to this conference I will hear God. We box Him into an event; it needs to happen at this place and this time. I can only hear when I'm in this environment. It doesn't work like that. He is speaking all the time, every time. You just need to be aware of Him.

Job 33:14 'For God speaks once or twice yet no one listens.'

I want you to imagine it like this. God speaks once or twice when He's speaking to you. If you get a dream but you didn't understand the dream, He doesn't stop there. If He realizes you didn't get it or you forgot the dream, He will find another way to get the message to you. You'll be driving in your car and you'll hear something on the radio and suddenly you remember you had a dream. You get to work and your unsaved boss will say something to you and you remember you just heard that on the Christian radio. That's God talking to you because He's going to talk through many different channels to make sure you hear it.

Have you ever been reading something and right after you read it, you go somewhere and you hear the same scripture in a whole different place? Then you go somewhere else and it's the same scripture again. Don't brush that off, that's God saying, 'I'm talking to you! The reason you keep hearing the same thing over and over again is because you were not listening the first time.'

What do you think recurring dreams are? If you keep having the same dream again, that's God saying, 'You're not listening! I need you to find out what this dream means so this dream can stop. There's a message in here that you're not heeding.' That's a recurring dream, it will stop happening once you hear the message and do the message. Then you can move on from that point. You will never have that dream again once you get the interpretation of the dream and do what God wants you to do.

So God doesn't need a special place or time to speak with you. He can do it anywhere and at anytime and through anyone. The more aware you become of His presence the easier it will be for you to pick up on what He's saying to you.

The last thing that can affect how you hear God is a difficult one, your *desire*. The thing that you want most and that you hang onto the most in life can sometimes affect how you hear God. If God has another message that doesn't line up with it, you reject the voice of the Lord and you tell yourself that it can't be God because this is it, when in actuality the whole time it's really you just wanting it so badly that every message that you receive is like a confirmation that you're right.

James 4:1-3 'Where do you think your fighting and endless conflicts come from? Don't you think that they originate in the constant pursuit of gratification that rages inside each of you like an uncontrolled militia? You crave something that you do not possess. So you murder to get it.'

Think that sometimes murder is not physical murder. It's what you tell yourself. You say things to kill off everything else that goes against what you want.

You want it so badly that everything and every message from God that you hear says yes to you, but it's not God. It is your desire. Yes, and while the bible says that God gives us the desires of our heart, the problem is when that desire is attached to your flesh or your soul that hasn't been renewed. Everything we desire should be viewed or filtered through the eyes of God.

The most powerful prayer you pray is,

'God align my desires with your desires. Make the things that I desire in life be what you desire for me to have. I don't want to desire anything outside of your will.'

When you live in that place, where all you want is what He wants for you, you can't fail! And sometimes this can be a very painful thing because we'll end up giving up things we want to remain in God's will. But you know what? It's OK because in the end, His plan is much better than ours and our finite mind cannot even begin to comprehend how amazing His plan is for us.

Jeremiah 29:11"For I know the thoughts that I think toward you, says the Lord, thoughts of peace and not of evil, to give you a future and a hope."

The pain of the surrender is temporary and ends once He unveils His plan to us. It is in these moments that we see how silly we were to hang on to some of the things we thought were so great.

As Job says, *'though He slay me, yet I will serve Him.'* This means either way, I get it or I don't, I'm still going to worship God. Whether He gives me what I want or He doesn't give me what I want, I'm still going to worship God.

If you approach things from that angle, it's going to be harder for your desires to get a hold of you because your heart will be to surrender to His will for your life.

How do you know when you've been drawn away into your own desires and it wasn't God? It's simple. It didn't happen. The thing you were so sure God said, never happened, and then you sit and examine it and you realize that you wanted it more than what you were willing to hear God about it.

The only reason I tell you this is because I've lived it. This was one of my earlier lessons when I was about 2 years old in the Lord. I was so sure it was God until it never happened. Then I told Him, 'Lord, I don't want to doubt Your voice in the future because I was so sure this was going to happen. I need you to bring me back to a place where I can really trust what I'm hearing. I trust You, but I don't trust what I'm hearing anymore because I was wrong about this.'

That's when the Lord started to teach me that your desires can give you a wrong message. Before you decide to hold on to something so tightly, you need to ask the Lord what He has to say about it. Before you wrap your emotions and your heart around it, you need to ask God to tell you what He thinks. You need to hear it from Him yourself. 'God, You need to tell me what You are saying about this.'

It is so much easier for you to hear when you haven't emotionally connected to it, when you don't care either way what He has to say about it, (though He slay me, yet I will serve Him) God can talk to you because your desire has not over ridden His voice in your life.

1 John 2:17 NIV "The world and its desires pass away but whoever does the will of God lives forever."

If you do the will of God you will always end up in a good place. You will be far happier, even though in the moment when you have to surrender your desire it may not feel like it. If you align you desires with anything else in this world, it's going to be gone one day.

It's all about what He is saying.

Matthew 6:21 "For where your treasure is, there your heart will be also."

Your heart is wrapped up in what you treasure the most. Therefore, let your desire be to do the will God. So that your treasure is in Jesus Christ and Him only. Trust in Him only; lean not on your own understanding. He will show you the right way.

This is a hard one, especially if you're already on the path of the desire. You might think, 'Oh, my gosh, I'm not sure this is God but I want it so badly. 'How do I back out of this?'

You have to let it go or you're not going to hear God at all. Before you invest your heart, your energy, your time, and your emotions in anything, you need to first go to the Lord God and ask, 'Is this You? Is this what You want for? me?' Then you'll be able to hear Him. Then you are in control of the decision to walk away without getting your desires wrapped up in it.

***

Personal Reflections:

We renew our mind, body, soul and strength by reading the word of God. How will you commit to scheduling time in the word?

Have you identified any issues you need to settle with the word of God?

Is there any area in your life where you see that you may have engaged in syncretism? Here is a prayer of repentance for you.

Abba Father, forgive me for engaging in _____. I pray that You will forgive me for sinning against You in this manner. I pray that You remove this and any evil spirits that are associated with it from my life. Continue to cleanse me from all these practices and show me any other areas where I may be engaging in this. Thank you for putting me back on the right path to hear Your voice, in Jesus name, Amen.

God talks to us anywhere, anyhow, any time. We should be able to connect with our Father along those guidelines; while watching a sunset, while cleaning the bathroom, gardening, while driving, anywhere and anytime. Has God spoken to you in a place that wasn't a church? Or through someone who wasn't even a Christian?

Unfortunately, greed and selfishness are rampant in our societies. We even have a phrase for it, 'keeping up with the Jones'.' Material things are not what make us happy, at least not for very long. Our desires should never be wrapped up in material things. Checking in with our Lord and Savior and being thankful for all you have will keep this at bay.

***

Prayer:

Abba Father,

Thank You for speaking to us Your children. I repent for any way in which I have turned to man, idols, images or any other source that was not You. I pray You forgive me and bring to mind any areas in my life where I am still walking in this sin. I pray You would clearly help me to discern the source for every message that I hear. Allow me to recognize Your voice quickly so that I will not go down the wrong path. Thank You for purifying what I hear with Your Word, in Jesus name.

Amen.

***

Chapter 5

How To Maintain The Voice Of God

*H*ow do you continually hear from God on a daily basis? This is really important because you can meet somebody that's saved and they have an experience with the Lord. They can clearly tell you about the time they heard from the Lord, but then you hear the same story over and over again every year or every two years. This means that nothing new happened. It happened at the very beginning of their relationship with the Lord, but somehow there was a bit of a drift that happened, and they haven't heard from God since. It's a one-time ordeal, an event, and it never happens again.

I don't want that to happen to you, once you tap into hearing the voice of God and hearing from God, I want this to be something that you experience on a daily basis. And it is very much possible. Yes, God does speak, and He speaks a lot. He wants to speak to every single one of His children. As I said before, being able to talk to God and having Him talk to you is not a spiritual gift, it is your right as a child of God to hear from your Father, and He does want to speak to you. This all comes through your relationship. It is not about anything else but your relationship. The people who hear from God on a regular and consistent basis are hearing because of their relationship with God.

Church is very important, however; I will tell you that Christianity is really more about your relationship with Him. So the vertical is the most important, before the horizontal. The horizontal is your relationship with other people, your relationship with your own family, and your relationship with your church family. The horizontal is starting a church or a ministry. While we do it to serve God, ministry is more about your horizontal relationships. But if the vertical relationship isn't right, which is the one between you and God, and then the horizontal will fall apart too. I don't want you to fall into the trap of thinking that your relationship with Christ has to do with your relationship with the church because the two things are actually different. They're separate. A lot of people go to church every Sunday. They sit there and they can have an experience with the Lord inside the church. The problem is the minute they leave the church, that's gone. What happens then is they believe that God only exists in that building over there. He only shows up when the worship team is singing or when the pastor is preaching or the priest does this or we have communion. That's when they experience God.

If that is how you build your relationship with God, the minute that gets taken away, as in Covid-19 lockdown and you're at home, you can't go to church, then your whole relationship with the Lord gets affected. Therefore, the horizontal relationship is one that is more external and seen by others while the vertical is internal and only exists between you and the Lord.

Your experiences with God should not just be kept in a church family. You should be having that at your home or wherever you are because you are really the church, you are the temple of the Holy Spirit and He resides in you and His communication is with you and through you.

When you become a Christian and start going to church on a regular basis, you are going to meet some people who say they are Christians, but they won't necessarily act like Christians or they may not treat you as you would expect to be treated. You can end up being hurt. Then what some people do is they say, 'I tried it, Christianity, and it doesn't work for me' or 'I turned away from the church because of what happened to me at church'. And it's understandable. But your relationship is with Him first, so once that is shored up and secure and that foundation is set right, it is less likely that you will walk away when something happens with others who may be in the church, even if it is a church leader. We know that we each have our own mind, body, soul, and spirit. And when we don't work on our soulish issues and regenerate them by the Word of God, then someone that has been saved for many, many years and may not even look saved, could turn around and hurt other people. Because of that you need to make sure you're stable and secure in your relationship, the vertical relationship with the Lord first.

Maintaining the voice of God is not a one-time deal and I want you to know that. He wants to talk to you every day. So how do you maintain it? You maintain it through your relationship. You know how they say, 'It's not what you know, it's who you know.' It's really true. It's who you know; God.

God will do things for you just because of you. Yes, He will. The word of God tells us in

Acts 16:31 'You will be saved, you and your entire household.'

Well, how does that work? He starts off with one person in that household. That one person is going to be you, if nobody else around is saved. You end up developing a really strong relationship with the Lord and through prayer He is going to talk to you and lead you in how you are going to reach the other people in your family.

So, it starts with one person, and then it flows through everybody else in the family. That's the whole idea. He wants to develop that relationship so that others can be saved, your own family members, and other people around you, in your workplace or your neighborhood or wherever you go. Through one relationship, many times, God will do things because one of us, you and I, will ask Him and He will do it. We see that with Abraham in

Genesis 18:16-32 " Then the men rose from there and looked toward Sodom, and Abraham went with them to send them on the way. And the Lord said, "Shall I hide from Abraham what I am doing, [18] since Abraham shall surely become a great and mighty nation, and all the nations of the earth shall be blessed in him? For I have known him, in order that he may command his children and his household after him, that they keep the way of the Lord, to do righteousness and justice, that the Lord may bring to Abraham what He has spoken to him." And the Lord said, "Because the outcry against Sodom and Gomorrah is great, and because their sin is very grave, I will go down now and see whether they have done altogether according to the outcry against it that has come to Me; and if not, I will know."

Then the men turned away from there and went toward Sodom, but Abraham still stood before the Lord. And Abraham came near and said, "Would You also destroy the righteous with the wicked? Suppose there were fifty righteous within the city; would You also destroy the place and not spare it for the fifty righteous that were in it? Far be it from You to do such a thing as this, to slay the righteous with the wicked, so that the righteous should be as the wicked; far be it from You! Shall not the Judge of all the earth do right?"

So the Lord said, "If I find in Sodom fifty righteous within the city, then I will spare all the place for their sakes."

Then Abraham answered and said, "Indeed now, I who am but dust and ashes have taken it upon myself to speak to the Lord: Suppose there were five less than the fifty righteous; would You destroy all of the city for lack of five?"

So He said, "If I find there forty-five, I will not destroy it."

And he spoke to Him yet again and said, "Suppose there should be forty found there?"

So He said, "I will not do it for the sake of forty."

Then he said, "Let not the Lord be angry, and I will speak: Suppose thirty should be found there?"

So He said, "I will not do it if I find thirty there."

And he said, "Indeed now, I have taken it upon myself to speak to the Lord: Suppose twenty should be found there?"

So He said, "I will not destroy it for the sake of twenty."

Then he said, "Let not the Lord be angry, and I will speak but once more: Suppose ten should be found there?"

And He said, "I will not destroy it for the sake of ten." So the Lord went His way as soon as He had finished speaking with Abraham; and Abraham returned to his place."

God went to Abraham and told him what he was about to do before he did it. God did this because of the relationship He had with Abraham. And, He will do the same with you.

If you continue to read the story you will see that Abraham with this information was able to negotiate with God to save his nephew Lot and was able to get word to Lot to leave the city before the destruction came.

Due to the nature of his vertical relationship with God, Abraham was able to help someone from his horizontal relationship.

Exodus 32:9-14 "And the Lord said to Moses, "I have seen this people, and indeed it is a stiff-necked people! Now therefore, let Me alone, that My wrath may burn hot against them and I may consume them. And I will make of you a great nation."

Then Moses pleaded with the Lord his God, and said: "Lord, why does Your wrath burn hot against Your people whom You have brought out of the land of Egypt with great power and with a mighty hand? Why should the Egyptians speak, and say, 'He brought them out to harm them, to kill them in the mountains, and to consume them from the face of the earth'? Turn from Your fierce wrath, and relent from this harm to Your people. Remember Abraham, Isaac, and Israel, Your servants, to whom You swore by Your own self, and said to them, 'I will multiply your descendants as the stars of heaven; and all this land that I have spoken of I give to your descendants, and they shall inherit it forever.' "So the Lord relented from the harm which He said He would do to His people."

The Israelites were saved based on Moses' relationship with God.

We see it again with Jesus

John 2:1-5 On the third day there was a wedding in Cana of Galilee, and the mother of Jesus was there. Now both Jesus and His disciples were invited to the wedding. And when they ran out of wine, the mother of Jesus said to Him, "They have no wine."

Jesus said to her, "Woman, what does your concern have to do with Me? My hour has not yet come."

His mother said to the servants, "Whatever He says to you, do it."

In the first miracle that Jesus performed where His mother, Mary, told him the host ran out of wine and asked Him to do something. Jesus was not happy about the request, saying that His time had not yet come. But He did it anyway, because of the relationship He had with her.

The Lord will do things for you when you ask based on your relationship with Him, how much time you are spending with Him.

Your cell phone goes off every week, well mine does, and it says you've spent this amount of screen time for the week; this is how much you've been on this screen. Your usage of screen time has gone up by 5%, or it's gone down by 10%. You can see all the hours you spend on your cell phone or your mobile device, your IPad. Let me ask you this, when it goes off and you see how many hours you've been doing that, I hope you are going to be able to say yes, and I have also spent 6 hours with the Lord this week, or seven hours with the Lord, maybe you can say I spent 20 hours with the Lord this week.

We shouldn't be spending all that time on a device looking at things and then not have time for the Lord. We have to schedule that time in somewhere. I know, sometimes in our daily lives, things change. So if you are in lockdown or quarantine, you may have more time on your hands now. What happens is later you may have to go back out to work and you may need to rearrange some things because that time that you used to have during the day is not there anymore, so you have to reschedule and reshuffle some things in order to make the time. It's your schedule; it has to be redone to make time for God.

Waiting upon the Lord is exactly as it says; it's waiting upon the Lord. It's sitting in silence. You shouldn't be afraid to sit and spend time with the Lord. Be conscious of it, not having your mind wander off, but just sit there and focus. Just imagine that He's right there in front of you and you're focusing on Him and He will speak to you. You need to make a discipline out of it. Where you can be in solitude and it doesn't scare you, silence shouldn't scare you. God loves it when you actually take the time to wait for Him to speak.

I'm going to share my first encounter with the Lord with you because when you get into the habit and the practice of doing this, of spending time and waiting for the Lord, it will happen. One of these days you are going to end up with an encounter. Yes, an actual encounter with Jesus Christ. Not just hearing Him speak but having an actual encounter.

Yes, it still happens today. It's not just left in the bible from years ago. He's still meeting with people today and talking to His children. But, again, it starts with knowing God.

I want to share a verse with you about knowing God.

John 17:3 'and this is the way to eternal life, that they may know you, the only true God and Jesus Christ, the one You sent to earth.'

So the way to eternal life is to know God. The key to your relationship is knowing God. What does that word 'know' really mean? It is not, 'I know God because I go to church' or 'I know God because I have a Masters of Divinity degree, or I studied and went to Bible College.' That's not the knowledge this is talking about. It is from the Greek word 'guinsoco' which means to come to know, to recognize, to perceive, to know through personal experience, firsthand acquaintances. Whoa! To know God though firsthand acquaintance. Think about that for a second. To experientially knowing God. To know Him through firsthand experiences. If you think about it, if it was really just about reading your bible alone, that wouldn't be enough to give you a firsthand experience. That means somewhere in your walk with the Lord, you're going to have an encounter with God. He is going to show up, He's going to talk to you, and you will probably say, 'Oh, my gosh, is this really happening?' Yes, because He wants to give you *that* level of knowledge. This is not head knowledge. It's an actual encounter and a firsthand experience with Him.

I'm telling you when that happens to you, you will never walk away from the faith. You will never give up on it because that's when you are going to say, 'I know God because I've experienced Him, I've encountered Him.'

Let me share my first encounter. I wasn't looking for this because I didn't come from a church environment where they talk about this kind of thing. My church was more of a 'you get to know God by reading the word' type of church, which is true but there is more to it than just that. But listening to this definition of the word 'knowing' God, it's more than just reading the bible. There is an encounter that happens when you truly get to know Jesus Christ in the way that I'm talking about, experiencing Him firsthand.

Firsthand experience starts with salvation and then it continues with your relationship. What you don't want is a relationship like some couples where you start off really good then you get married. Then you have kids and then your whole relationship becomes about the children and you don't pay attention to each other, just the children. You have all these years with the kids and then they move out of the house. Now you are sitting there with a complete stranger going, 'Ummm, who are you?' You know the husband is saying this to the wife, and the wife is saying to the husband, 'I don't know who this man is' because there has been this distance because the kids were in the middle. Sometimes we do that, put the church in the middle. It's a building. It's not the actual relationship with Jesus Christ. You have to work on your relationship with Him by spending time with Him. It's like any other relationship. Spending time in prayer, reading the bible, and sitting in silence waiting for Him. Then it happens.

For me, that's where my journey with God began, just being in prayer. I remember I would take the whole Saturday to be with the Lord. I would do everything in silence so that I could listen. I would talk to Him, and then I would be silent. I would read the word and I would spend hours and the Lord would be talking to me. It was glorious!

When I started reading the word, I wanted to do nothing more than read the bible, sit on my bed and just read, the entire bible. When I got saved, I didn't tell my friends right away, so they would still call and ask if I wanted to go to the club on Saturday. I would tell them not this Saturday. I have something that I'm doing. Then they would ask if I wanted to go on Friday. I told them I was busy on Friday, too. That was okay the first weekend, but the following weekend they wanted to know his name. Because people generally don't go to the clubs every weekend and then suddenly stop unless something changed. And, they assumed I must've met someone and was spending time with him instead of going out. I really should have said, 'It's Jesus' but I didn't. All I wanted to do was to sit in my room and read my bible. That's all I wanted, just to talk to Him, and spend as much time as possible with Him because the more time I was with Him, the more He was talking to me, the more he was revealing things to me.

This went on for a few months; I think 7 or 8 months but I really don't remember how long after, because I wasn't writing it down so I don't remember exactly when it happened but it was within the first year that I was saved. Honestly, I never thought about having an encounter. I didn't even know this was possible. One night I was going to bed, I had to work the following morning. I read the bible and turned off the light. I just laid there with my eyes closed but I see Him coming through my bedroom door. He has His floor length white robe on and He walks in and He comes around to the side of my bed. He sits down on the bed right by where my knees are. He is sitting down right by my knees and I can feel the bed go down where He sat. My eyes are closed, but I am seeing Him.

He's sitting there and He turns and He starts talking to me. I'm talking back to Him. I think I went to bed around 11:00pm. I'm talking to Him and He's talking to me, just going back and forth, talking, and talking. He had been there for a while and I opened my eyes and turned to look at the clock. It said it was 1:15am, I had one of those digital clocks that show the numbers in red and it lights up in the room so I can easily see the time. I didn't see Him while my eyes were open but my bed was still pressed down, so I knew He was there. I closed my eyes and turned back and we were talking some more. We're laughing, whatever He was saying was funny, we were going back and forth and I was laughing and laughing. We started talking about other things and I started crying. I mean I was crying to the point that my pillow was wet. I'm crying and we're talking some more. I know the time is going so I open my eyes and look over at the clock again; it was a quarter to two. I close my eyes and we continue talking and once again I look over at the clock and now it's 2:15. The clock is going and we're talking and talking and it gets to be around 4:00. I think to myself I have to be up at 6:00 in the morning because I have to work. I close my eyes for the last time and I said to Him, 'I want to keep talking to you but I have to get up in the morning. I'm going to be really tired in the morning, if you can make it so that when I wake up, I feel like I had 8 hours of sleep. I want to keep this going, I don't want to stop talking to you but I'm going to be tired, so just make it so that I feel like I've had a full night's sleep. So He continued talking but I didn't bother looking at the clock anymore because I knew it was okay, he's going to do it just as I asked of Him. We're talking and laughing and crying, there were many different emotions happening. It felt like for the night we had gone through a range of emotions. Finally, we get to the end. I know we got to the end because He then pulls this thing out of his robe that looks like a scroll. He rolls it open and He has a pen in His hand, you know like an old feather pen, and He's writing on it. When He gets done writing, He rolls it up, like a tube and He turns around to me on the bed and he takes this scroll by one end and He pushed it into my heart, just down into my chest. And He says to me, 'Everything that we've just discussed is written in there and it is in your heart. If you want to know anything about where you are in life and what is going on, all you have to do is ask me, and I will tell you.' I said, 'Okay.' He got up and He walked out of the room. I turned to look at the clock. It was 6:00, my alarm went off.

I sat up in the bed and to tell you the truth it felt so surreal I wondered to myself if this really just happened. I touched my pillow and sure enough it was wet still from the tears. The interesting thing is that I can't remember a single word of our conversation other then when I asked Him to make me feel like I slept for hours and when He said it's all written in my heart. I cannot remember anything else that was discussed.

And I was refreshed. I felt like I slept for 8 hours except I hadn't slept for the whole night! We talked for the entire night! It was like, 'WOW, that was something else!' I knew then that He was really telling me about my life and what would happen. That certainly explains all the emotions I was feeling based on all the things we discussed. I never told anybody about it because I was a new believer. You know the kind of church that I go to, they would be like, 'Really, that happened? Huh, so where's that in *the bible?*' Well, it turns out it is in the bible.

Psalm 139:16 "Your eyes saw my substance, being yet unformed. And in Your book they all were written, The days fashioned for me, When as yet there were none of them."

Psalm 56:8 NET *"You keep track of my misery. Put my tears in your leather container. Are they not recorded in your scroll?"*

Psalm 40:6-8 "Sacrifice and offering thou didst not desire; mine ears hast thou opened: burnt offering and sin offering hast thou not required. Then said I, Lo, I come: in the volume of the book it is written of me, I delight to do thy will, O my God: yea, thy law is within my heart. "

It's your scroll. The bible talks about our scrolls and He's written it in our hearts and every day of our life before we even lived one day has been recorded. He knows what it is and He was telling me that it is also inside of me and all I have to do is ask Him if I'm not sure what I'm supposed to do, where I'm supposed to go. 'Ask me and I will tell you.' That's all He was saying. Those emotions of the laughter and the crying and everything else in between, were really Him telling me my life. Believe it or not, this is what is going to happen. That is just how much He cares, to speak with us, to have a conversation with us. And it's not just me. It's in the bible which means it is for you as well. It's all of us, and He wants you to know. The question is, do you want to know Him? From this kind of relationship that I'm telling you about, you are going to hear very clearly from Him.

While your first encounter may not be like mine, it might be something completely different. I don't want it to just stop at one for you. It's not once for me, I just told you the first one. It happens all the time. And this is the kind of relationship Jesus wants to have with you.

Personal Reflections:

What manner of getting to 'know' God are you going to add or increase in your daily schedule?

Will it be reading His word? Have you ever really *read* the bible? Have you taken a book of the bible and read it from beginning to end, got to know the people involved, understood their lives?

Will it be praying or talking to God? Will you be talking to God while gardening, while driving down the road, while sitting by the fire pit as the sun slowly sets, while rocking your children or grandchildren to sleep?

Will you be listening to God? Are you one of those people that turn the TV or the radio on as soon as you are out of bed in the morning? Is the first thing you do every morning is check your phone? Do you have silent time during your day? Do you enjoy communing with nature?

***

Prayer:

Abba Father,

Help me to know You better. Show me how and when I can make time to spend with You. Write Your will upon my heart and bring me into a full knowledge of You, Your desires, and the purpose You have for my life. As I commit to spending time with You, help me to understand what it is You have planned for me. Reveal to me what You have written in the scrolls about me. Grant me security in my steps as I journey towards You, in Jesus name,

Amen

***

Chapter 6

At The End Of The Day

I want to leave you with 2 final thoughts based on questions I get asked when I teach Christians how to hear from God.

First, one of the main questions I've heard from others is "What if it's not God but the devil that is speaking to me?"

I want you to know that that question is rooted in fear. And it's not the good kind of fear of awe and reverence to God but the one that leads to a place of torment.

1 John 4:18a "There is no fear in love; but perfect love casts out fear, because fear involves torment."

You must know that your Father in heaven would never lead you to a place where you're talking to a demon because He loves you. His perfect love for you should remove every doubt that this could ever happen. The minute you get a revelation on how deeply He loves you, this thought will leave you. And, you'll want to do nothing more than to connect with Him.

The truth is from reading the bible I don't see anyone that was afraid of talking to a demon when they went to God. Therefore, this shouldn't be a concern to you.

There's no precedent for this happening in the word of God.

The next thing you need to know is that demons or evil spirits are not omnipresent. What that means is that they cannot be in more than one place at a time. The question then is why would there be a demon in your house? And, if there is one, then you should be working to get rid of it. You shouldn't be afraid to connect with the Lord while continuing to allow an evil spirit to take up residence in your home.

Most Christians don't have a demon in their house so most Christians will have no problem connecting with the Lord through the principles taught in this book.

The second question I get asked is, "What if I get the message wrong?" What if I misinterpret what God is saying and make the wrong decision?

Can this happen? Yes. You're human and you'll get some things wrong but how else are you going to learn how to get it right? It's like riding a bike. You may fall off once or twice but after awhile you learn what to do and what not to do.

How do you think I found out that your desires can give you a false message? I fell off the bike. But that only happened once. From it I learned a valuable lesson that I can now teach you. It was painful when it happened but I am grateful for the experience because now I know. It also helped me to discern when others are prophesying out of their own desires. It had a purpose.

At the root of this question I find that this is about never wanting to suffer, to never experience pain. We hope that if we can hear God clearly and we walk in complete obedience we will never have to go through trials, pain and suffering. We hope that if we can get it all right we'll bypass suffering, we'll never end up with 'egg on our face', we'll get it right above everyone else, and we get to be the hero.

But, no matter how well you hear God, you'll still go through some things. This is how you grow.

James 1:2-4 "Brethren, count it all joy when you fall into various trials, knowing that the testing of your faith produces patience. But let patience have its perfect work, that you may be perfect and complete, lacking nothing"

This is how you go from glory to glory. It is a part of our process. If you never made a mistake you would be perfect, and in heaven, not here on earth having to endure with the rest of us.

As hard as it may be for you to hear this, sometimes God will actually make you take a route just so that you can learn a lesson.

Yes, you'll get it wrong sometimes. When you get to that place where you need to make a decision and you're not sure which way to go, instead of being stuck, do what you feel God is asking you to do. Move forward in faith. I want to share with you the one scripture that has always brought me peace and comfort.

Romans 8:27-28 "Now He who searches the hearts knows what the mind of the Spirit is, because He makes intercession for the saints according to the will of God.

And we know that all things work together for good to those who love God, to those who are the called according to His purpose. For whom He foreknew, He also predestined to be conformed to the image of His Son, that He might be the firstborn among many brethren."

God searches your heart and He knows you had good intentions when you made that decision, even if the decision was wrong. At that moment, Jesus is making intercession, prayer, for you in heaven according to God's will so that you will get back on track if the decision was the wrong one.

And, what's even better is that He takes all those mistakes and He turns them into something good. He makes it beautiful. Even the bad decisions you made. Even the ones you made that you knew were wrong!

He knew from before you were even born what your destiny and purpose is and He makes sure that at the end of the day it will all work out for good.

If you love Him, at the end of the day, you are going to be just fine. You will get to your destination.

At the end of the day you will be victorious, and you will win.

Blessings

***

ABOUT THE AUTHOR

N icole Murray is the author of *How To Start A Prayer Ministry* as well as the founder of Missionaries Of Prayer, a non profit organization that promotes prayer worldwide. In

her role as a teacher and mentor of prayer, she has reached worldwide audiences ministering through the gift of prophecy and prophetic intercession while winning many souls to Christ. Her passion for reaching the poor, both in the natural and in the spirit, has led her to do worldwide missions to many countries sharing the love of Christ while ministering to the natural and spiritual needs of the people. Ms. Murray hosts numerous prayer workshops and seminars nationally and internationally as well as online. Her non profit ministry not only ministers to people in English but also in Spanish.

For more information visit

www.MissionariesOfPrayer.org

CPSIA information can be obtained
at www.ICGtesting.com
Printed in the USA
BVHW060449050521
606425BV00006B/1409

9 781737 045403